TRUE SELF,
TRUE WEALTH

PETER COLE, ChFC, LCSW, *and* DAISY REESE, LCSW

TRUE SELF, TRUE WEALTH

A PATHWAY TO PROSPERITY

Foreword by Price Cobbs, MD

ATRIA BOOKS
New York London Toronto Sydney

ATRIA BOOKS
A Division of Simon & Schuster, Inc.
1230 Avenue of the Americas
New York, NY 10020

BEYOND WORDS
PUBLISHING
20827 N.W. Cornell Road, Suite 500
Hillsboro, Oregon 97124-9808
503-531-8700 / 503-531-8773 fax
www.beyondword.com

Editor: Julie Steigerwaldt
Managing editor: Lindsay S. Brown
Copy editor/proofreader: Jennifer Weaver-Neist
Illustrations: Elizabeth Collentine-Cole
Cover design: Jeanne Lee, Atria Books
Interior design: Carol Sibley
Composition: William H. Brunson Typography Services

First Atria Books/Beyond Words trade paperback edition October 2007

ATRIA BOOKS and colophon are trademarks of Simon & Schuster, Inc.
Beyond Words Publishing is a division of Simon & Schuster, Inc.

For more information about special discounts for bulk purchases, please contact Simon & Schuster Special Sales at 1-800-456-6798 or business@simonandschuster.com.

Manufactured in the United States of America

10 9 8 7 6 5 4 3 2 1

Library of Congress Cataloging-in-Publication Data:
Cole, Peter H.
    True self, true wealth : the new psychology of money / Peter Cole and Daisy Reese.
      p. cm.
    Includes index.
    1. Finance, Personal—Psychological aspects. 2. Money—Psychological aspects. 3. Wealth—Psychological aspects. 4. Self-actualization (Psychology). 5. Conduct of life. I. Reese, Daisy. II. Title.
HG179.C658   2007
332.024′01—dc22

2007004397

ISBN-13: 978-1-58270-178-3
ISBN-10:   1-58270-178-4

The corporate mission of Beyond Words Publishing, Inc.: *Inspire to Integrity*

We dedicate this book to our parents and our children with love and gratitude.

CONTENTS

ACKNOWLEDGMENTS

There are many people we want to thank. Our appreciation goes to Elizabeth Collentine-Cole who did a fabulous job with the graphics. Thanks to Reese Minshew for brilliant editorial help when we needed it most, and to Alex Reese for valuable input. To Ananda Reese and Hannah Collentine-Cole—our appreciation for your unfailing support and understanding. Our journey continues to be supported by the loving guidance of our teachers: Taj Inayat, Gayan Macher, and Blanche Fleur Macher. Thank you for all you have given us. Thanks to the folks at our broker-dealer, Securities America Inc., especially Bob Binn for doing such an incredible job, day in and day out. Thanks to Cynthia Black and Richard Cohn at Beyond Words Publishing, whose passion and vision we admire. Thanks to Joan Cole and Bob Wendlinger whose support for this project has been invaluable. Thank you to Price Cobbs who was generous in many ways. A heartfelt thank you to Andrea Hurst at Andrea Hurst Literary Management, without whom this book would never have come to fruition.

FOREWORD

Throughout my professional career in medicine, I have always wanted to read a book of practical and insightful financial advice specifically aimed at people in my profession. Nowhere in my extensive training to become a physician and a psychiatrist was any part of the curriculum devoted specifically to the making, spending, and saving of money. Early in my educational journey, visions of money making floated in and out of my consciousness and even (perish the thought) fleeting thoughts of attaining some level of affluence. But, after finishing internships and residencies and incidentally generally weighted down in debt, there were few, if any, venues for fruitful discussions about how to get on a pathway to prosperity. I was joining the noble profession of healing, and the idea of thinking and talking directly about money was tarnishing to the mythology that made doctors special. As my experience broadened, I realized that many of my colleagues in other fields, be they lawyers, firefighters, social workers, or educators, had their own built-in barriers about money making and thus comparable aversions to pouring as much of their intellect and emotions into their finances as they did into their professions.

Here at last is a book designed for the person who chooses to work consciously with the many issues, beliefs, and patterns that are involved in achieving financial success. Peter Cole is a Chartered Financial Consultant and a

psychotherapist with many years experience in both fields;
Daisy Reese is a skilled and experienced psychotherapist.
Their previous book, *Mastering the Financial Dimension of Your
Practice*, was a groundbreaking treatment of money issues in
professional mental health practice. In *True Self, True Wealth*
they have written a book for everyone on the psychological,
spiritual, and practical aspects of building wealth. They
detail the steps you must take, both emotionally and practi-
cally, to put your life on the pathway to True Wealth.

True Self, True Wealth takes you on a journey of self-
discovery—historical, emotional, and spiritual. The authors'
wide-ranging experience in psychotherapy provides a deep
understanding of the ways in which people change and grow.
Peter's brilliance in financial planning allows him to speak
clearly and specifically to the financial challenges of each life
phase, guiding you through the maze of choices toward the
goal of an abundant and satisfying life. Daisy's wisdom as
a psychotherapist provides the emotional grounding for
achieving that prosperity.

Everyone who grows up in a family absorbs both overt
and covert messages about money. In later life these messages can trigger behavior that undermines your best efforts
at making wise decisions. Through working with the exercises outlined in the first half of this book, Peter and Daisy
provide powerful tools to understand your feelings,
unconscious patterns, and self-defeating behavior. You will
develop the power to take charge of your life and move
toward the goals you have set for yourself. This lays the
groundwork for the second part of the book, which deals
with the practical steps necessary for financial success.

We live in a free enterprise system that offers enormous
opportunity. At the same time, however, it requires us as
individuals to assume the major responsibility for our own
economic well-being. Health care, higher education, and
security in retirement are important considerations for
every individual and family. *True Self, True Wealth* offers a guide

to understanding the choices available in the financial realm, assessing the needs of yourself and your family, and making decisions based on your enlightened self-interest.

In reading this book, you will find yourself enthralled and challenged by the many parts of yourself you will be asked to explore. Most of all, however, you will feel that you are walking down an unfamiliar road with wise and trusted guides. The authors are dedicated to providing their readers with the tools of transformation. By the time you complete your work with *True Self, True Wealth* you will have enhanced your self-awareness, increased your confidence, and developed your financial competence, and you will be ready to deal with money matters from a new and empowered perspective.

—Price Cobbs, MD
CEO of Pacific Management Systems
Author of *My American Life, Cracking the Corporate Code, Black Rage,* and *The Jesus Bag*

INTRODUCTION

How do you define financial success? Each person has goals and values that are quite personal. Your vision of True Wealth may be very different than anybody else's. It is, after all, a reflection of your own True Self. Perhaps you have a vision of a more comfortable home, a great education for your kids, or simply a better understanding of proper money management and investing. Whatever your image of True Wealth, it can be within your grasp.

As we move through school, we are trained in many different skills, but rarely are we taught how to deal with money. Many of us go through our whole lives playing it by ear and then don't realize until we're close to retirement that we haven't planned sufficiently. This book is meant to break the cycle of ignorance. We invite you to take an exciting journey with us to financial knowledge and empowerment. Your journey will pay dividends in personal and spiritual growth that go well beyond financial reward, for it is in developing your own True Self that you find True Wealth.

In this book you'll find the support you need to move toward your vision of True Wealth with courage and commitment. Having consulted with scores of diverse people about their finances, we have come to an understanding about the ways in which money, psychology, and spirituality are intertwined. The Buddhist saying "How you do

> The beginning is the most important part of the work.
> ~ **Plato**

anything is how you do everything" applies to money. How you live your life and how you view yourself are reflected in how you relate to money—how you make it, save it, spend it, invest it. Becoming more empowered and financially successful requires knowledge of both yourself and investing.

Many people dedicated to spiritual development have lived their lives with the misconception that financial cares are superficial and that any concern for money is somehow "unspiritual." However, as Ram Dass has said, it is necessary to "honor this incarnation." To live fruitfully in this world and contribute to the well-being of others, it is necessary to work responsibly with your finances.

> In dreams and in love there are no impossibilities.
> ~ Janos Arany,
>   Hungarian Poet

Our physical, mental, spiritual, and economic selves are inextricably linked. Think of money as a form of energy that continually flows in and out of your life. If you dam it up with psychological blockages, you stop the flow. By unraveling your feelings and patterns surrounding money, you can allow money to flow in and out and create balance in your financial life. *True Self, True Wealth* is a roadmap to guide you toward a sophisticated understanding of (1) your relationship to money and the role it plays in your life, (2) the spiritual and emotional meaning of money in your life, and (3) strategies for successful money management and wealth-building throughout the life cycle.

We have divided *True Self, True Wealth* into two sections. Part 1, "True Self," deals with the emotional and spiritual dimensions of your prosperity. You will learn about your individual financial psychology. As you deepen your understanding of yourself and untangle your old patterns, unhealthy feelings, unconscious blind spots, and your money script, you will become more empowered about money. Your financial decisions will become better informed, less emotionally driven and will serve you better.

Part 2, "True Wealth," gives you the guidance you will need to move toward prosperity with wise and empowered action. We'll explore the Six Pillars of True Wealth:

1. Smart Investing
2. Home Ownership
3. Empowered Earning
4. Conscious Spending and Credit
5. Adequate Insurance
6. Wise Planning

True Self, True Wealth provides an integrated, emotionally connected approach to your financial empowerment. Our purpose is to support you in transforming your emotional, spiritual, and practical relationship with money. We give you the right tools to create real, lasting financial success for you and your family. Once you have learned the basics of the Six Pillars you will have the information you need to intelligently implement your plan for financial success.

> It is our interpretation of money, our interaction with it, where the real mischief is and where we find the real opportunity for self-discovery and personal transformation.
> ~ Lynne Twist, Writer

Why a Psychologically Informed Money Book Is Necessary

Even if you have a practical knowledge of money and investing, it is still very possible to make bad money decisions if you do not understand your money psychology. We have seen otherwise well-informed investors make foolish financial decisions due to their emotional blindspots. For example, an otherwise brilliant psychiatrist (yes, psychiatrist!) got caught in a co-dependent relationship with a man who gambled away her very substantial life savings. Although she had minored in business as an undergraduate, and understood the basics of investing, her emotional blind spots caused her great financial harm. To help you avoid being blind-sided by your emotions around money, we have dealt very seriously with the psychological material in this book. We give you the tools you need to succeed.

Money packs a powerful emotional punch. It affects not only individuals but also families—and its legacy continues through the generations. No matter how much or how little your family had, money played a powerful role in shaping your family history. In a world where so much is defined by money, it can hardly help but be a significant theme in family life. What were your family's rules around money? How did your family define success? What were your parents' financial goals for themselves and their children? As you answer questions like these, you will begin to define your money script—a set of negative feelings and beliefs about money that were absorbed during your childhood and continue to shape your behavior in adulthood.

Based on over twenty-five years of practicing and teaching psychotherapy and financial planning, we have identified ten money scripts. As you identify the script that best describes the emotional baggage you carry from your early experiences, you begin the process of making new choices and creating a new relationship with money.

> Change takes place through awareness and active choice-making.
> ~ Joseph C. Zinker, PhD, Psychologist

Why an Emotionally Informed Money Book Is Not Enough

Working through money scripts and healing your relationship with money will create a sense of empowerment in your financial life. We cannot stop there, however, because resolving emotional blocks and old scripts is only useful if you know how to apply yourself effectively to life's financial challenges. At this point, the task shifts to taking action to meet your investment and other financial challenges. The applied chapters in this book—the "True Wealth" section—provide you with the necessary tools to do exactly that.

First you will learn the basics of sound investing. We teach you, in simple terms, the difference between various asset types such as stocks, bonds, and real estate. You'll learn about the science behind diversifying and properly allocating your assets—Modern Portfolio Theory, created by

Nobel Prize–winning economist Harry Markowitz. This leading theory among investment professionals today will allow you to invest with consistency, discipline, and intelligence, avoiding many of the most common mistakes.

Next, we look at home ownership, where you will learn how to save thousands of dollars and enjoy the many benefits of this investment. We explore the subtle interplay between how you feel about yourself and the amount of money that you earn. You will acquire the tools to increase your value to your clients or your employer, to value your own worth, and to negotiate to get the money you deserve for the work you do. We then proceed to spending issues, teaching you how to spend consciously and how to take care of your emotional needs with outlets that meet those needs and don't drive you into debt. You will also learn valuable tools for managing debt.

Regardless of how wisely you invest, you must take steps to safeguard the wealth you accumulate. While smart investing is like playing offense in the investment game, adequate insurance coverage and estate planning are the defensive part of your game. You will learn these skills in the last chapters of the book. These areas are vital so that you and your heirs do not see all that you have worked for eaten up by either disaster or the tax collector.

> **The Six Pillars of True Wealth**
> 1. Smart Investing
> 2. Home Ownership
> 3. Empowered Earning
> 4. Conscious Spending and Credit
> 5. Adequate Insurance
> 6. Wise Planning

It's Time to Grow—in Wealth and Wisdom

We have spent thousands of hours working with clients as psychotherapists and as professional financial planners, discovering how each field relates closely to the other. We offer you information that is not only financially sound but also deeply grounded in well-established psychological theory. If you put these principles into practice you will see marked changes in your psychological response to money, you will experience less anxiety around money issues, you will be a better money manager, and you will be well on your way to creating True Wealth.

We're excited to embark on this journey with you. As you strengthen your Economic Self, may you gain in wisdom, creativity, and connection to Spirit.

We don't receive wisdom; we must discover it for ourselves after a journey that no one can take for us or spare us.

~ Marcel Proust, Writer

PART I
TRUE SELF

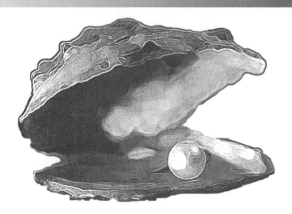

YOUR ECONOMIC SELF

I

Who are you? This may sound like a ridiculously simple question, but in this chapter we ask you to consider the answer in depth.

Your Self operates in at least four dimensions. To be a happy, healthy human being, it is important to pay attention to each of these dimensions:

- Physical Self
- Emotional Self
- Spiritual Self
- Economic Self

Your Physical Self is exactly that—your physical body. To function well, it requires proper nutrition, fresh air, exercise, and sufficient rest. Your Emotional Self is that part of you that responds with feelings to the people and situations you encounter each day. This is the "you" that needs to be understood, to give love, and to receive love. Your Spiritual Self lives in the place where you connect to humanity, the world, and the universe—it responds to beauty and includes your higher purpose in life. Your Economic Self is the part of you to which you may have paid less attention. It connects you to the world of money and financial dealings.

The purpose of this book is to help you enhance the health of your Economic Self. This Self is engaged in issues

> Each today, well-lived, makes yesterday a dream of happiness and each tomorrow a vision of hope. Look, therefore, to this one day, for it and it alone is life.
> ~ Sanskrit poem

such as building your career, investing, making your cash flow work, managing your spending and debt, planning for retirement, and dealing effectively with the many relationships that affect your financial well-being. This dimension of Self can suffer from wounds caused by damaging scripts and roles originating in childhood. We call these damaging scripts money scripts, and in chapter 4 you will identify the script that comes closest to describing your relationship with money. Through understanding your Economic Self and your money script, you become empowered in your financial life. With this knowledge, your Economic Self is able to participate in the free-flowing exchange of financial energy—and it is toward this end that this book is dedicated.

Whether your Economic Self is able to function at full capacity depends partly on you. One critical component is wishing, or daydreaming. Just as making love is a function of your Physical Self, so is wishing a function of your Economic Self. For lovemaking to be pleasurable and satisfying, it is certainly not necessary for it to lead to the birth of a child. For wishing to be pleasurable and satisfying, it is not necessary for it to be based in reality or to lead to a specific action. You can look at wishing as a way to open up your creativity and widen your horizons. It's true that "wishing doesn't make it so," but it's also true that "if you don't have a dream, it's hard to make your dreams come true." Your wishes themselves can have transformative, alchemical power—if you nurture them.

You're almost ready to begin the first exercise, which involves daydreaming. In preparation for that, however, it's important to digress for a moment to talk about the Superego and Superego Attacks, which may try to sabotage your progress.

Superego Attacks

What do we mean by the Superego? In this context, it refers to the voice of the punitive or critical "parent" that plays

> Imagination is more important than knowledge.
> ~ **Albert Einstein**

and replays itself in your head. It may be the voice of an actual parent, a grade school teacher, Little League coach, clergyman, or some other symbolic figure from your childhood. You can easily recognize this voice because

- it is invariably negative;
- it criticizes without offering any alternatives;
- it attacks rather than supports your efforts;
- it leaves you feeling helpless and ashamed.

Superego Attacks usually strike when we are feeling most vulnerable—when we're trying something new, taking a risk, or being open about our feelings, for instance. If we don't take quick action, a Superego Attack can paralyze us and prevent us from progressing.

Like all bullies, the Superego likes to persecute the timid but quickly backs down when met with a powerful response. Depending on your own style (and the style of your Superego), you can use various types of responses:

- Humorous—"Thanks for sharing. I love you too."
- Fiery—"That's enough! Cut it out!"
- Dismissive—"Yeah, yeah, here we go again."

Regardless of which approach works for you, the act of responding strongly to your Superego will, over time, make it less and less destructive. A strong response will also help the vulnerable part of you feel protected and safe enough to continue risking.

With all of the above in mind, let's proceed to our first exercise. Throughout this book we will be suggesting that you journal and do various exercises. We recommend that you buy a composition book (like you had in school as a kid) and call it your "Money Journal."

> What is this self inside us,
> this silent observer,
> Severe and speechless critic,
> who can terrorize us
> And urge us on to futile activity
> And in the end, judge us
> still more severely
> For the errors into which his
> own reproaches drove us?
>
> ~ T. S. Eliot

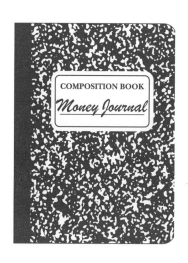

COMPOSITION BOOK
Money Journal

Exercise 1: Your Images of Financial Well-Being

In your Money Journal, draw four images of your wishes for financial well-being. The objective here is to let your mind freely explore the images without getting caught up in efforts to do it "right" or make it "beautiful." Your drawing ability is not the issue here. It's much more important to let yourself experiment and enjoy the process. If you should start to feel self-critical, just refer back to the mechanisms for dealing with Superego Attacks earlier in this chapter.

> Destiny grants us our wishes, but in its own way, in order to give us something beyond our wishes.
> ~ Goethe

Susan's images of financial well-being

Exercise 2: Financial Well-Being in Words

Now that you have come up with images of what your financial well-being might look like, let's use language to explore your wishes further. Take some time to write about what you have drawn. You may want to write simply or creatively. You may even want to write a short story or poem about your pictures. Remember, this is just for you. Let yourself be abbreviated, whimsical, humorous—whatever strikes your fancy. One way to approach this exercise is to finish the following sentence in five different ways: *Whether or not it is realistic, one thing I wish for in my financial life is . . .*

Now you have put your wishes into both words and images. These will be useful to refer back to as we move forward.

Exercise 3: Ideal Qualities of My Economic Self
While you're still in "wishing mode," let's consider what qualities you'd like to possess as part of your Economic Self. For example, Peter would like to possess the qualities of leadership, clarity, vision, and strength, in addition to great negotiating skills.

In your Money Journal, list the qualities that would ideally be integrated into your Economic Self. The objective here is not to critique yourself for what you think you lack or to rush to "fix" things. Just allow yourself a few moments to savor the ideal Economic Self you are envisioning. Here are some qualities our workshop participants came up with, just to get you thinking: seriousness of purpose, generosity, frugality, thoroughness, toughness, follow-through, and discipline.

Money and Its Emotional Meaning

As with many of the most significant things in life, money is both concrete and symbolic. Therefore, we must work with money on both its concrete and symbolic levels. On the concrete level, money is the agreed upon medium of exchange for an almost infinite range of economic activity. Whether it takes the form of paper dollars or available credit on your charge card, money is what makes the buying and selling of goods and services possible. To deal effectively with money on the concrete level, it is necessary to understand and respect the rules inherent in economic life. We will be exploring these in depth as we proceed through the book.

The symbolic aspect of money is equally important. To deal confidently and effectively with money, we must gain an understanding of the role it played in our families of origin, the emotions it stirs, and its impact on our self-perception. When we present "True Self, True Wealth" workshops, we ask participants to brainstorm about what feelings arise when they hear the word "money." Their feelings

> Ideals are like stars; you will not succeed in touching them with your hands. But like the seafaring man on the desert of waters, you choose them as your guides, and following them you will reach your destiny.
> ~ Carl Schurz

about money run the gamut—from excitement to shame to anger to envy. When you begin to bring these strong feelings to conscious awareness, you become much better able to understand and contain them, rather than being ruled or undermined by them. Awareness allows us the freedom to act in our own enlightened self-interest rather than being overwhelmed by emotions such as anxiety or guilt.

Economic Well-Being

What is economic well-being? Is it measured by your bank balance? The size of your investment portfolio? Your career success? Certainly, all these things impact your economic well-being. Most of us (with the exception perhaps of Buddhist monks!) need some degree of economic success and security to feel a sense of well-being. That degree, however, can vary dramatically from person to person. Some people are quite content to live barely above a subsistence level—finding satisfaction in living simply in material terms. On the other hand, many people with inherited wealth or highly lucrative careers find themselves overwhelmed by feelings of guilt, anxiety, envy, or ennui in dealing with financial matters.

To meaningfully explain economic well-being, we must refer back to our earlier discussion of consciousness awareness. A sense of economic well-being requires the following:

- Becoming aware of your emotional reactions to money
- Becoming aware of your values and priorities
- Making a conscious choice to contain and work with your emotions
- Making conscious lifestyle choices that allow you to express your values in the way that you live

The Paradoxical Theory of Change

At this point, you may feel yourself beginning to mobilize internally: "OK, if that's what it takes, I can do it." You're

> The symbol is neither abstract nor concrete, neither rational nor irrational, neither real nor unreal.
>
> ~ Carl Jung, Psychiatrist

right. You certainly have the capacity to make real and lasting changes in the way you deal with money. This change cannot happen by force of will, however. Before you can get where you want to go, you must take a clear and non-judgmental look at where you are now.

The Paradoxical Theory of Change (from Gestalt Therapy theory) tells us that true change must begin with the discovery and acceptance of "what is." As you patiently and compassionately explore where you are in your dealings with money, you will see more and more clearly the path to where you want to be.

Self-help books, especially those on money, often give the impression that change is simply a matter of discovering the "right solution" or "just making up your mind." Offering this sort of advice seems similar to the ads that promise "weight loss while you sleep," or "magic pill reverses effects of aging." Real change, in any area of our lives, is a growth process requiring time and commitment. We must till the soil before the seeds of change are planted. Then we must continually water and fertilize the soil, weed and work the garden before we enjoy the bountiful harvest.

> The art of living lies less in eliminating our troubles than in growing with them.
> ~ Bernard M. Baruch, Financier

Object Relations

If acknowledging "what is" is the first step of change, developing an understanding of our history and its impact on us is an important next step. One of the most effective ways to develop this understanding is through exploring our object relations. This term refers to the relationships we developed in our early life—with parents, siblings, and other major players. Because these early relationships are so primary and intense, they color the way we view ourselves and the ways in which we relate to others throughout our lives.

Let's look at an example that involves feelings about money. Jean grew up in a family where the men (specifically her father) controlled the money. Jean's father was the CEO of a successful company and controlled the money at home in the same domineering fashion. As a child, Jean felt dismissed and powerless in dealing with money. All her wants were catered to, but she was never taught to balance a checkbook, design a budget, or contribute to a savings account. She developed an object relation to her father in which he was dominant and powerful while she was helpless and incompetent. The combination of seeing her father as commanding and powerful while seeing herself as small and powerless is an object relation. By the time she was grown, Jean had transferred this object relation to money itself. Money became the stimulus to a feeling of being small and powerless.

As she began to work with the Paradoxical Theory of Change, Jean became aware that she had many negative feelings about herself associated with money. In an effort to understand these feelings, she started to explore her early object relations. She found that her feelings about herself in relation to her father had affected her feelings about dealing with any sort of financial matter.

Jean brought a sense of self-acceptance and curiosity to her work on her own object relations. Increasingly, she became able to experience her feelings, associations, memories, and body responses to money matters without anxiety or self-criticism.

As she worked through her feelings and responses to money, she began to see many things more clearly. She identified her money script (which we explain in chapter 4) and the corresponding actions that would put her on the pathway to True Wealth. She started to understand her father's fearfulness about money and how he tried to shield her from his insecurities. What had felt to her like "control trips" had been a way for him to deal with his fears. Further, she began to see that her feelings of powerlessness were a natural response in her childhood to her father, but these feelings were not helpful to her as an adult. She found herself developing a heightened capacity to tolerate

> What is *is* and one thing leads to another.
> ~ Erviny Polster,
>   Psychologist

her anxiety when dealing with financial issues. Gradually, Jean began to change the way she viewed herself in relation to money.

Money and Emotional Intelligence

Emotional intelligence refers to the self-awareness that comes from exploring our issues with an open heart and mind. Jean came to a new understanding of her object relations around money. She developed a greater capacity to tolerate and work with her own anxiety. She developed a better understanding of her father, and this gave rise to greater compassion for him. All of these were big steps on Jean's journey toward emotional intelligence around her money issues. She found the courage to face her money issues and made great progress toward achieving her financial goals, as we will see.

> What is necessary to change a person is to change his awareness of himself.
> ~ Abraham Maslow, Humanistic Psychologist

Choice-Making

Because of her overwhelming anxiety, Jean had avoided dealing with or even looking at her financial accounts. It had been months since she had opened a statement from her broker. Now, because of the emotional intelligence she had developed around her money issues, Jean was prepared to take the next step. She started to mobilize her financial self and she took smart, informed action to gain control of her financial life.

Jean committed to going over her statements each month. This seemingly small act laid the foundation for further action. She now has regularly scheduled meetings with her financial planner and has implemented a new asset allocation for her investments, putting 25 percent of her earnings into her various investments. In addition to updating her insurance and adding better disability coverage, she regularly balances her checkbook. She also took action at work and successfully negotiated a long overdue raise with her boss.

Jean's journey is an example of the power of the Paradoxical Theory of Change. Rather than berating herself for her struggles or trying to force herself to "be different," she allowed herself to move through a natural process. She developed an understanding of her difficulties, learned about her money script, made a series of conscious choices to act courageously in her own best interests, and is now implementing a thoughtful and effective financial plan.

We must make the choices that enable us to fulfill the deepest capacities of our real selves.

~ Thomas Merton,
    Trappist Monk, Writer

THE SPIRITUAL DIMENSION

2

It has been said that we are not human beings on a spiritual journey, but rather spiritual beings on a human journey. The human journey demands that we honor not only our spiritual wings but also our material roots. Thus, putting our house in order on the material plane is a vital aspect of our spiritual development. There is an unfortunate perceived disconnect in our society between the pursuit of wealth and the pursuit of spirituality. The options are so constricting. We're told we can choose to have a rich, developed, spiritual life at the expense of all material comforts. Or we can pursue wealth at any cost and develop a life that is physically satisfying but devoid of spiritual connection.

When the subject of material wealth comes up among people interested in the spiritual aspect of life, it is often dismissed as being "maya" or illusion. Alternatively, it can be condemned as "the root of all evil." Certainly, to become totally immersed in the mindless accumulation and hoarding of wealth is not conducive to spiritual growth. To prize money above all else, to judge others on the basis of their economic status, or to succumb to the dictum "just look out for number one" will certainly result in a life that is emotionally and spiritually impoverished, regardless of material success. But what is the alternative?

There is another way to navigate the choppy waters that connect money to Spirit: building wealth can be an integral

> Honor this incarnation.
> ~ Ram Dass,
> **Spiritual teacher**

part of spiritual development. How we act in the economic realm—how we handle money—is equally as important as how we treat our partners, raise our children, or care for the natural world.

There are three major components of a healthy spiritual practice:

> I am a part of all that I have met.
>
> ~ **Lord Tennyson**

1. A strong relationship to the Self—the ability to view your current, physical incarnation with a clear and compassionate eye
2. A strong relationship to others—feeling deep connections, giving and receiving support
3. A strong relationship to Spirit, or the recognition that we are all one

Building wealth—in a conscious, thoughtful way—strengthens all of these relationships. It supports your relationship with yourself through helping you truly work with your incarnation. And using money as a barometer—not as a measuring stick—can help you develop a deep sense of your own worth and worthiness.

There is no question that the Self of this incarnation must create a healthy relationship with money in order to thrive. The author and philosopher Ken Wilbur has written eloquently about the different levels of reality. According to his model, at one level there is no duality, only unity. There is no substance, only energy. At another level, however, there is indeed duality. (If I eat all the apple pie, there will be none left for you.) At this level, substance is very real. (If I treat an oncoming car as merely energy without substance, the results can be disastrous.) When we are working on a spiritual level, concepts such as nonduality, infinite resources, matter as energy, and so on, are very relevant. However, when dealing with the *physical* level of daily life, we are called upon to respect its demands and limitations.

On the spiritual level, money is simply energy. Like any form of energy, money itself is a morally neutral force. The force must be directed and controlled by its user here on the physical plane. After all, money doesn't care if it is used on bullets or bread. It is equally willing to buy crack cocaine and destroy young lives as to purchase building materials for Habitat for Humanity. To use the energy of money wisely, it is necessary to develop maturity and the ability to use power in this incarnation. And this maturity and awareness reflect our growth.

There are certainly plenty of examples of the dangers of not utilizing this opportunity for growth. Young rock stars, inheritors, and lottery winners often suffer from "sudden wealth syndrome." Financial success that is achieved too soon or too suddenly can be debilitating. Just as a six-year-old can be dangerous behind the wheel of a car, one who is emotionally and spiritually undeveloped can be dangerous when given too much money.

> Capital as such is not evil; it is its wrong use that is evil. Capital in some form or other will always be needed.
> ~ Mahatma Gandhi

As well as helping you develop the ability to use power wisely, money helps to keep you grounded. There has been much talk lately among spiritual teachers about the dangers of the "spiritual bypass," which happens when people become so enchanted with the highs of meditation and spiritual teaching that they become reluctant to do the difficult developmental work that will allow them to sustain the high states. Rudolf Steiner, a nineteenth-century mystic and founder of Waldorf Education, stated, "For every step in spiritual development, a person must take three steps in moral development." These steps in moral and emotional development include development on the physical plane. This means paying attention to the Physical Self, the Emotional Self, and the intellectual self. Your Economic Self plays as vital a role in your development as the other aspects of your life.

Additionally, money can be a useful tool for recognizing your own inner worth. This is treading on dangerous ground—we certainly wouldn't want to equate your net worth with your value as an individual—but we've seen money act as such an amazing tool for personal empowerment. Two of our children are self-employed, and we had the opportunity to watch them really work through evaluating prices for their services. We saw how frustrated they became before they fully recognized the worth of the work they were doing . . . and saw how frequently others undervalued their services because they themselves were blind to their own skills. We also got to see their growing self-respect as they began to take their work seriously, and charge reasonable prices for their services.

Take your own valuation seriously as well. As the poem "Desiderata" states, "You are a child of the Universe. No less than the trees and the stars, you have a right to be here." Once you realize the truth of this, you can relax into the flow of life. You know at the deepest level that life offers you abundance. Does this mean that you can forget about investing wisely or taking out a needed insurance policy? Can you just sit back with the assumption that "God will provide"? Of course not. Remember that with increased awareness comes increased responsibility. It is certainly necessary to develop your Economic Self—to find your "right livelihood," manage your money well, and reach out to those less fortunate. However, you can do this without anxiety or unnecessary worry. You can trust that if you do your part, that is all that is required of you. "Going with the flow" does not mean sitting idly and letting the river carry you. Rather, it is incumbent on you to pay attention to how the river is flowing and steer your boat in accordance with that flow.

To steer your boat well, you have to have a clear sense of where the rapids are. In chapter 4 we will be looking at money scripts, which are developed from all the messages absorbed about money over the years. Working with your money script is a way to develop not only your Economic

We are not human beings on a spiritual journey, but rather spiritual beings on a human journey.
~ Teilhard de Chardin, French Jesuit Priest, Philosopher

Self but also your Emotional Self. Learning about investing and managing your money will stimulate you intellectually. Attuning to the flow of life and doing your best to move in concert with it is a deeply spiritual practice.

As you develop all the aspects of your Self, you will become more and more the person you were meant to be. The purpose of self-development is not to become some prototypical "perfect" being. Rather, it is to unfold fully into your authentic self. We each have a part to play in the grand symphony of life. Exploring your values, dreams, family history, and the strengths and challenges of your Economic Self leads to a deeper understanding of yourself. This understanding, in turn, enables you to live your life from a place of self-awareness and interconnectedness. You can allow yourself to be as wonderful as you really are. In the words of Marianne Williamson:

> What a man can be, he must be. This need we call self-actualization.
> ~ **Abraham Maslow**

We are born to make manifest the glory of God that is within us. It's not just in some of us; it's in everyone. And as we let our own light shine, we unconsciously give other people permission to do the same. As we feel liberated from our own fear, our presence automatically liberates others.

Williamson wisely notes that our own ability to become fully and authentically ourselves has a profound effect on others. Money plays a part in this as well. When we work toward the maturity and self-awareness that building wealth requires, we become freer to develop sustaining, loving, intimate relationships with others.

The knowledge that you are capable of satisfying your own material needs does not lead to isolation. Rather, it allows you the ability to stand on equal footing with partners and friends. You become someone who wields considerable power in this world—and someone who is capable of using this power is a self-actualized, responsible way.

Exercise: Living Authentically

It's time to get out your Money Journal again. Take a moment to look back over the work you have done in your journal so far. Once you have refreshed your memory, just sit quietly for a few minutes with your eyes closed and contemplate the following questions:

- What would living my fully authentic and empowered life look like?
- What would I need to change in my life to foster my authentic power?
- Is there a small step that I can take now toward greater authenticity and empowerment?

When you feel ready, write or draw your responses to these questions. Your responses don't have to be linear, and they don't need to make sense to anyone but you. Don't labor over the exercise. If you find you don't have an intuitive response to one or more of the questions, just jot down the responses that do arise in you. As you move through the book, you may well find that you wish to come back to this exercise and expand on your first responses.

Charitable Giving

To deal successfully with money, you need to appreciate and experience both the spiritual and material aspects of it. To ignore the spiritual aspect leads to a life that may be comfortable on the material level but devoid of meaning. To ignore the material aspect is to invite a slap in the face from reality—"that which doesn't go away, even when you ignore it." But once you begin to take ownership of this work and build your connection to it in a healthy and positive way, you become a powerful individual in this reality. With this power comes, of course, responsibility. As you find your financial life improving and your connection to others deepening, it is imperative that you foster change in the global sense as well. Connecting to others implies connection to people you've never met and will never see. This is where philanthropic giving comes in.

> Twenty years from now you will be more disappointed by the things you didn't do than by the ones you did do. So throw off the bowlines. Sail away from the safe harbor. Catch the trade winds in your sails. Explore. Dream. Discover.
>
> ~ Mark Twain

All the major religions emphasize the importance of expressing gratitude for our blessings through some form of giving back to the world. Christians avow that "it is better to give than to receive." The Jewish faith speaks about *tikkun olam*, the obligation to help heal the world. Muslims place great importance on *adab*, dealing with others with courtesy and kindness. And Buddhism preaches "loving compassion" for all sentient beings. One aspect of honoring the spiritual dimension of money is channeling money-energy toward good works: practicing philanthropy. Does being a philanthropist require funding large projects or giving away huge sums? Not at all. In fact, when broken down to its Greek roots, philanthropy simply means "the love of mankind." This love can be expressed in a myriad of ways, depending on your circumstances and inclination.

> Is the rich world aware of how four billion of the six billion live? If we were aware, we would want to help out, we'd want to get involved.
> ~ **Bill Gates**

You might want to sponsor a child in a third-world country through Save the Children. You might want to make a donation to the Sierra Club to help with environmental protection. You might want to volunteer to make audio books for the blind, or donate your carpentry skills to Habitat for Humanity. Whatever you decide, the size of your contribution is less important than the fact that you are contributing. As our children's school says in its annual campaign letter: "When you contribute, even a few dollars, you are saying 'yes' to the goals and ideals of the school." When you contribute, even a small amount, to the world, you are saying "yes" to humanity and creative evolution.

A word to the wise: No matter how pure your intentions or how lofty your aims, it is still necessary to respect the inherent rules of fiscal reality. For several years we have been members of a group of wealthy, socially conscious philanthropists. Individually and collectively, the members of this group make a significant impact on the world. For the most part, they use their money wisely, generously, and to maximum effect. Each year, however, a small number of members disappear. They let their generosity overrule their enlightened self-interest and simply give away all (or at least way too much) of their money. No longer are they able to support the causes they so strongly believe in. No longer are they able to affect the world through the wise use of their resources. By giving in to a generous impulse, they have, in effect, robbed themselves of their potency.

A Balanced Approach to Money

Here is an opportunity to contemplate your own approach to money and recognize where you may be out of balance. Ask yourself the following questions:

> We make a living by what we get, but we make a life by what we give.
> ~ Winston Churchill

- How attuned am I to the energetic flow of money?
- Do I bring in enough money to live comfortably?
- Am I able to be good to myself financially without guilt?
- Do I feel rich enough to share with others?
- Am I able to respect the power of money without being intimidated or consumed by it?

As you consider your answers to the questions above, you will begin to get a picture of what aspect of money is summoning your attention. Continue your self-evaluation with these additional questions.

- Are you a person who tends to dismiss the power of money, considering it beneath your notice as you focus on "higher things"?
- Do you rely primarily on "positive thinking" and "visualizing abundance" to manage your financial affairs?

If either (or both) of these descriptions applies to you, chances are that your focus has been on the spiritual aspect of life. Your strength probably lies in a conscious connection to the universal whole and an ability to attune to the subtler, nonmaterial realms. Your task is to acknowledge the sacredness of the ordinary; the most mundane details of daily life can be infused with beauty and even holiness. The key is simply paying attention to those details rather than ignoring or dismissing them. On the other hand:

- Do you often find yourself caught up in the daily struggle to succeed, losing sight of your higher purpose?
- Do you find it difficult to trust that, if you do your part, your needs will be met?

If these descriptions depict your mindset, it may be that you cope well with the practicalities of life. "Taking care of business" may come naturally to you. Your task is to step back a little—relax, let go, and trust in the essential loving-kindness of the universe.

As you can see, the goal is to develop a balanced approach to money (and indeed to life!). By honoring both the physical and spiritual aspects of money, we move toward a truly satisfying life, which offers the experience of self-support and interconnection. And moving toward this life is the highest homage that we can pay to Spirit—it is the beginning of the journey toward unity.

The mystics have voiced it from time immemorial. Quantum physicists and cosmologists are now working with scientific evidence of it. Pictures of the earth shot from space show one aspect of it. Whether you talk about the Big Bang, the Body of Christ, the One Being, or the Brother-hood of Man, you are talking about the essential "oneness" of all life.

It is interesting to visualize the individual's path to enlightenment as being like the two hands circling a clock face. We start out in a state of perfect unity (12:00) and become gradually more and more individuated until we reach 6:00. At this point we feel ourselves to be a distinct and separate individual. However, as Richard Olney, the

> It is a kind of spiritual snobbery that makes people think that they can be happy without money.
> ~ Albert Camus,
> **Writer, Philosopher**

founder of Self Acceptance Training, said, "The greatest wound to the spiritual body is the illusion of aloneness." If we are to complete our journey toward true maturity, we must traverse the other side of the clock face, moving gradually toward a sense of unity with the whole. As we begin this second half of the journey, there is a paradigm shift. No longer do we view ourselves as isolated individuals. Rather, we are able to cherish our uniqueness while understanding that we are embedded in the whole of humanity and indeed the whole of life. We are not, and cannot be, self-sufficient. Nor can we avoid affecting others with our actions and with our presence.

The journey toward wholeness is not one that can be accomplished once and for all. We will always have times of challenge, regression, alienation, and fear. But once we have had a taste of the fulfillment that comes with working through our issues, we can come back to the place of wholeness more readily as we mature in the spiritual dimension of our financial journey.

> To have abundance, we need only to consciously receive what has already been given.
> ~ **Sufi saying**

MONEY, YOUR FAMILY, AND ECONOMIC INDIVIDUATION

3

Insight into your Economic Self begins with an exploration of your family's economic history. Your Economic Self is deeply affected by generations of family history to which you are heir. This economic history encompasses your lineage's struggles, challenges, triumphs, and losses with work and money. It is the historical narrative of how your family made their way in the world, and the emotional impact of that history on each member of the family. Your family's economic history works powerfully in the background of your money consciousness, and colors everything that you think, feel, and do in your economic life.

Why does it matter to know your family's economic history? Because you already know this information in your bones, and it influences the way you think and feel. But you may not know it consciously yet. Conscious awareness gives us choice and empowerment. If you want to feel economic empowerment, you must have Economic Self-knowledge, and that begins with knowing your family's history with money.

Let's begin our exploration with an exercise to bring memories of your father, mother, and grandparents into relief.

> In every conceivable manner, the family is the link to our past, bridge to our future.
> ~ Alex Haley, Writer

Exercise: Exploring Your Family History

To trigger memories, it is helpful to put a picture of your father and his parents and your mother with her parents in front of you while journaling.

Write freely about your father's money experiences and attitudes first. Then do the same exercise with your mother.

Questions to Help Guide You

- What were your father's economic circumstances in childhood? Was his family rich, poor, or somewhere in-between?
- How did his parents define financial success?
- Did your grandparents consider themselves successful? Were they immigrants? Did they experience discrimination? How did the depression of the 1930s affect the family? Were there upheavals that affected the family financially?
- How did your father do financially compared with his siblings?
- What messages did your father absorb about money from your grandparents?

> If you cannot get rid of the family skeleton, you may as well make it dance.
> ~ George Bernard Shaw, Writer

In families some issues are discussed overtly while other issues are communicated covertly. Money issues are commonly communicated covertly. We, the authors, have found that covert communication is lodged most deeply in the family DNA. Covert communication about money gains its power precisely in the fact that its assumptions are never openly discussed. Like the force of gravity, covert communication is unquestioned and always exerts its influence. A simple example of an overt family rule is this: Johnny does the dishes on Wednesday and Mary does them on Thursday. A simple example of a covert rule is this: Don't ask Dad for money for that new dress for the homecoming dance; he has enough problems of his own and your needs will just upset him. The covert rules are the ones that really hold sway in most families.

Herein lies a basic psychological dilemma for us as children and ultimately for us as adults. These covert financial rules exert a powerful influence on how we think and feel about money and about our parents as economic actors. Most importantly, they go a long way toward defining our money script and limiting the awareness of our economic selves.

As you journal, you start to put words to deeply felt family history that has unconsciously shaped your money script and attitudes. We encourage you to explore hitherto unspoken history and to learn more about the forces that have shaped your Economic Self. Our goal in doing so is not to wallow in the past or to cast blame, but to expand your awareness of the forces that are at work so that you are freed up to make your financial choices more consciously.

Exercise: Remembering Holidays

For this exercise, it helps to find a picture of your family at Christmas or Hanukkah and have it near you as you journal about your family's holiday experiences.

Questions to Help Guide You

Put yourself back into what it felt like when you were a child during the holiday season.

- How did your family deal with the holidays?
- Were there pressures that you experienced in the family during this time—were there typical pressures that arose?
- What were the overt family rules about the holidays?
- What were the covert family rules about the holidays?
- Did your parents seem to get anxious about money during the holidays?
- Was love expressed through gift giving?
- What did your experience of the holidays tell you about your family's economic status?

> Holidays have no pits.
> ~ **Eugenio Montale,**
> **Italian Poet**

It's OK for You to Do Better than Your Parents Did

Although the American dream is to have our children do better economically than we have done, this is not necessarily the way all families operate. In many families the covert rule is that the children should not achieve a higher status than the parents. In some families there is a pull to keep each member in check. This pull protects the family from feeling humiliation around a perception of economic powerlessness. Sometimes the pull is to protect the family members from feeling abandoned by keeping each family member from individuating and leaving home. Other times there is abuse in the family that is kept secret, and family members are discouraged from finding much of a life outside the rigid social boundaries of the family.

Some families exert a strong pull for economic enmeshment. Individual family members are discouraged from discovering their own true economic selves. In emotionally enmeshed families, there is a great pull for each individual to adopt the family scripts about money and economic life. We cannot separate our economic lives from the rest of our lives because our economic lives encompass our work and our fundamental lifestyle choices. When the family exerts this kind of symbiotic pull in our economic lives, it has a stifling effect on the whole of our lives. Say, for example, that the parents in an economically powerful family exert their power in discouraging their son from pursuing a career in art. They use their emotional leverage to steer him to business school. He may find wealth in business but not true economic empowerment, for true empowerment comes from fully expressing your passion in the world.

> I think we pick up good vibes as well as the secrets. The family is my fate, it is also my grace.
> ~ John Bradshaw, Writer

Economic Individuation

In order to find true economic empowerment you need to leave home psychologically—no small feat. It requires that you fully examine the scripts and pressures your family exerted on you both overtly and covertly. It means that you recognize the ways love was expressed in your family of origin and find your own path to love and intimacy. It means that you find your passions in life and create the self-support to develop these interests into your own path to economic empowerment. Psychologists call this emotional journey away from home and into your own empowerment the process of individuation. Economically, individuation is a journey out of the scripts of the past into your own way in the world. It is a path of finding work that is both meaningful and economically rewarding. It means examining your money values and aligning your economic life with those values. It is a continual process of defining and refining your way in the world.

> There is only one success—
> to be able to spend your life
> in your own way.
> ~ Christopher Marley,
> Writer

GROWING BEYOND YOUR MONEY SCRIPT

4

Have you ever had the experience of hearing words come out of your mouth that made you sound exactly like your mother or father—words that you swore you'd never say? Have you ever found yourself deeply embroiled in a destructive relationship that feels like déjà vu? If you're nodding your head in recognition, you've had some direct experience with the power of the unconscious. Family messages, old patterns and habits, and suppressed fears and wishes can ensnare us before we know what's happening. Despite our intentions, we can find ourselves acting against our own best interests again and again. Willpower is no match for the unconscious. In order to avoid repeating the past, we must bring it into the light of conscious awareness. By understanding your history and exploring your unconscious needs, wishes, fears, and fantasies, you develop the ability to make choices based on present reality—choices that will truly serve you well.

In this chapter we introduce you to money scripts. We have all developed ways of dealing with money based on our early experiences and the messages passed on to us from our families. Based on the sum of these experiences and messages, we construct a money script, which defines our characteristic approach to money. The script we construct may have been necessary when we created it, but if we are to move toward

> Go on a journey from self to self my friend ... such a journey transforms the earth into a mine of gold.
> ~ Rumi, 13th Century Persian Philosopher

greater comfort and ease in dealing with money, we must relinquish our old patterns and allow our script to evolve.

Change begins with awareness. Knowing your money script can open the door to greater awareness of how your Economic Self developed, and the strengths and weaknesses you carry. We hope that you'll find working with the money scripts to be fun. At the same time, we know that looking uncompromisingly in the mirror can be difficult and sometimes painful. Now is the time to gather your courage. Your willingness to increase your self-knowledge holds the promise of a freedom that will surprise you.

Remember what you learned earlier about Superego Attacks in chapter 1. Working with your money script is a good opportunity to practice fending off those attacks. You deserve compassion. Give yourself credit for the hard work you're doing and don't demand perfection. You're entering into a process that (hopefully) will continue throughout your life. It will be challenging, but it can also be exciting and incredibly rewarding.

With each money script, we identify avenues for growth and integration; your script need not be a prison. Through awareness and self-acceptance you can move toward new growth. For example, the Masquerader tries to cover up his shaky self-esteem by posturing with money in ways that may undermine his economic well-being. As he works with these tendencies, he finds new ways to deal with his insecurities. He learns to love himself, to have compassion for his insecure side, and to create real and resilient economic well-being in his life.

The following pages contain descriptions of ten common money scripts. Following the description of each one, you will find a self-test in which you are asked to check off the characteristics that you feel apply to you. When taking the self-test, think of how you were as a young adult just out of school, before you'd had much opportunity to work on self-development.

> Your vision will become clear only when you can look into your own heart. Who looks outside, dreams; who looks inside, awakens.
> ~ Carl Jung, Founder of Analytical Psychology

The ten icons below represent the money scripts.

The Power Player

The Hoarder

The Victim

The Procrastinator

The Masquerader

The Prince or Princess

The Craver

The Gambler

The Coupon Clipper

The Co-Dependent

The Power Player

The Power Player feels that he lives in a hostile world. Having learned in childhood that he was exceptional (often from his mother) but also met with suspicion and competition (often from his father), the Power Player feels both entitled and under attack. This will often play out in a sense of entitlement. The self-talk from the entitled side of him says, "You are great and powerful." The self-talk from the vulnerable side of him says, "You are worthless unless you achieve great wealth and power." He is thereby caught in a struggle to attain ever more wealth and power.

Core Belief:

Others cannot be trusted. I have to be in charge.

Primary Emotion:

Anger—There is no justice except what power provides.

Secondary Emotions:

Fear—A hostile world is waiting to take away whatever is not well protected. Shame—Any vulnerability is something that must be well hidden.

Money Represents:

Power over others; parental power in childhood

Seeks Comfort by:

Trying to gain increasing control of money and power

Avenues for Growth and Integration:

Learning to recognize the underlying connection with others, and learning to value process over power; emphasizing the positive, protective aspect of his style over the controlling aspects

████████████████████████

Characteristic Self-Concepts of the Power Player

Check the statements that feel true for you.
If you check five or more, the Power Player is your money script.

___ I am the best person to be in charge of money issues.

___ I protect my family's money from a hostile world.

___ Other people might think I'm controlling about money, but I feel like I'm bringing needed strength to the situation.

___ I would rather fight a worthy battle, exposing my true friends and enemies, than have things go my way easily.

___ This world consists of winners and losers in the sphere of money. It's better to be a winner.

___ I feel contempt for weaker people who don't deal with money well.

___ If someone cheats me or is dishonest with me, I will avenge that injustice.

___ I don't mind conflict about money; it brings out my fighting spirit.

> The highest proof of virtue is to possess boundless power without abusing it.
> ~ Lord Macaulay,
> British Politician, Writer

The Victim

The Victim feels cheated with regard to money. Over-controlled in childhood, the Victim has a passive-aggressive streak. In childhood, he could not assert autonomy with his parents directly, so he asserted some control by *not* doing what was demanded of him. The Victim may have a tendency toward self-defeating financial behavior such as going into debt, not paying bills, or otherwise not taking care of his financial business. There is sometimes a general lack of self-care with the Victim and he can be difficult to help, as it sometimes seems like he is trying to prove a point with his self-defeating behavior.

Core Belief:
I've been cheated.

Primary Emotion:
Anger—Though the true anger is at controlling or abandoning parents, the Victim turns that anger inward in an unconscious attempt to show them how much he has been hurt.

Secondary Emotions:
Fear—I will be punished and left hurt and destitute. Shame—The Victim may be ashamed of his self-defeating position but is more locked into anger at others—and punitive self-defeating behavior—than he is bound by shame. He may in fact take a certain masochistic pride in his self-imposed victimization.

Money Represents:
The controlling, withholding parent

Seeks Comfort by:
Suffering

Avenues for Growth and Integration:
Dealing effectively with anger so that it is not retroflected (turned back in on the Self); learning to take responsibility for his own financial well-being and not blaming others

Characteristic Self-Concepts of the Victim

Check the statements that feel true for you.
If you check five or more, the Victim is your money script.

___ I have bad money karma—people do not give me what I deserve.

___ I would like to save, but it is just not possible right now. Maybe I will get started later.

___ Sometimes I feel so down I just don't care what my money picture is.

___ I will do what you tell me about money, but I will resent you.

___ My money situation will hurt you more than it hurts me.

___ It is someone else's fault that I am in my money situation; if I changed it would only let them off the hook.

___ I am tired of having others call the shots about my pay and money situation.

___ I can bear the suffering that comes from lack of money better than others could.

> It is possible to get out of a trap. However, in order to break out of a prison, one first must confess to being in a prison.
> ~ **Wilhelm Reich, Psychoanalyst**

The Masquerader

The Masquerader uses money as a vehicle for achieving self-respect and the respect of others. In his world there are winners and losers, and the Masquerader is always precariously close to feeling like a loser. This fear of loss compels him to cloak himself in the trappings of wealth. He is forever comparing himself to others. In his mind every relationship has a top dog and an underdog. Having been loved in childhood for what he could achieve rather than for his essential Self, he uses money to elevate himself and thereby make himself feel acceptable and lovable.

Core Belief:
Money and success bolster my self-esteem.

Primary Emotion:
Shame—He feels ashamed that his true financial picture is not acceptable to others or to himself. The Masquerader may, in fact, be very well-off financially, but still feel inadequate. He confuses success with perfection.

Secondary Emotions:
Fear—His underlying, poor financial self-esteem will be revealed. Anger—He is loved for his success rather than for his true Self.

Money Represents:
Winning the admiration of others

Seeks Comfort by:
Supporting the facade

Avenues for Growth and Integration:
Learning to accept his own fears and frailties with regard to money; learning to derive his financial self-esteem, not by comparing himself with an inflated idea of financial perfection but by accepting his humanness and imperfections; accepting himself and thereby making himself feel acceptable and lovable

Characteristic Self-Concepts of the Masquerader

Check the statements that feel true for you.
If you check five or more, the Masquerader is your money script.

___ I care what others think about my money situation.

___ Looking successful is very important to me.

___ Sometimes I feel down and scared about my money situation, but I don't let others see me sweat.

___ I am judged by what I produce financially.

___ I have high standards of others; I like to be around winning, financially successful people.

___ Sometimes I feel on top of the world about my money situation; other times I feel worthless.

___ I spend more than I should on "image" things like cars and clothes.

___ Saving is less important to me than getting things that make me feel good about myself.

> I am not in this world to live up to other people's expectations, nor do I feel that the world must live up to mine.
> ~ **Fritz Perls, Founder of Gestalt Therapy**

The Craver

The Craver tries to fill herself up with money. Not having had her needs met in early childhood, she uses money to satisfy them. She does not know how to express her needs directly, and frequently is involved in unfulfilling relationships. She may over-spend and splurge on herself in a vain attempt to take care of needs that can only be met through intimacy. Other Cravers will purposefully deny themselves of what they want and will feel deprived.

Core Belief:

Spending money fills me up when I feel unsettled and needy.

Primary Emotion:

Shame—Her needs were shamed in childhood, and her needs are now a source of shame for her.

Secondary Emotions:

Fear—Her needs for love and intimacy will be left unmet; she will be abandoned and destitute. Anger—Others do not consider her needs and seem to be self-centered. She feels passed over and has a chronic sense of low-grade anger and hurt.

Money Represents:

The fulfillment of unmet interpersonal needs

Seeks Comfort by:

Shopping and gift giving

Avenues for Growth and Integration:

To develop a healthy relationship with her emotional and financial needs; to develop clarity around the acting out of her emotional needs through spending if spending has become a substitute for meeting those needs

Characteristic Self-Concepts of the Craver

Check the statements that feel true for you.
If you check five or more, the Craver is your money script.

___ Shopping helps me soothe my anxiety and relieve my feelings of loneliness or emptiness.

___ I often spend more than I can afford without considering the consequences.

___ I can swing back and forth between the extremes of feeling very giving and very needy with money.

___ It is hard for me to find a middle ground between depriving myself and over-indulging myself with money.

___ I sometimes feel it is unfair that I am not being taken care of as I feel I deserve to be.

___ I can feel unappreciated and resentful when others take advantage of my generosity.

___ I sometimes feel angry and envious when others can afford luxuries that I would like to have.

___ It is easy for me to overextend myself by helping others too much financially.

> Land of Heart's Desire,
> Where beauty has no ebb,
> decay no flood,
> But joy is wisdom,
> time an endless song.
> —**William Butler Yeats**

The Coupon Clipper

A feeling of "never enough" besieges the Coupon Clipper; there is always the feeling that disaster lurks just around the corner. The Coupon Clipper is the product of a precarious childhood. Because her family was unable, for whatever reason, to provide her with a basic sense of security, the Coupon Clipper developed a heightened sense of financial instability. Her care and vigilance may lead her to curtail spending but can never bring her the sense of security she craves. Her task is to develop a sense of trust in both the flow of life and in her own capacity to keep her footing amid shifting currents.

Core Belief:
I am inches away from becoming a "bag lady," so I must save my pennies.

Primary Emotion:
Fear—She feels a loss of control, as if poverty is lurking right around the corner even when that is far from the truth of the situation. Saving pennies gives a sense of security, and there is a basic lack of trust.

Secondary Emotions:
Anger—Her parents did not convey a sense of security to her as a child. Shame—She tries to hide details about childhood poverty or other childhood struggles.

Money Represents:
A sense of control in a scary, chaotic world

Seeks Comfort by:
Bargain hunting and coupon clipping

Avenues for Growth and Integration:
To begin to develop some faith in the abundance of the universe; development of the capacity to trust

Characteristic Self-Concepts of the Coupon Clipper

Check the statements that feel true for you.
If you check five or more, the Coupon Clipper is your money script.

___ I like to keep my money readily accessible so that I feel in control.

___ It's important for me to feel like I spend carefully and wisely.

___ A good bargain is often more important to me than the best quality.

___ It is hard for me to look to others for advice or help with money management.

___ I like to think of myself as shrewd—someone who cannot be taken advantage of.

___ It feels almost sinful for me to spend money on my own pleasure or development.

___ I am critical of those I consider to be show-offs with their money.

___ I would much rather put a hundred dollars into my savings account than have a night on the town or a new outfit.

> Fear is not a bad place to start a spiritual journey.
> ~ Kathleen Norris, Writer

The Hoarder

The Hoarder is distinct from the Coupon Clipper in that the focus is on amassing more and more money rather than holding on tightly to what is already there. Like Dickens's Scrooge, he knows at his core that the world is an unfriendly place and that there can never be too much protection for himself and for those he loves. The message learned in early childhood was "better safe than sorry," and the Hoarder spends his life putting the bricks of his fortress carefully in place. Sadly, he often finds that the fortress, while providing safety, cuts him off from satisfying relationships and leaves him isolated. Only by allowing himself to step out from behind his walls—to expose himself to the joys and terrors of life—can he develop the sense of inner peacefulness he so vainly sought through accumulating financial riches.

Core Belief:
Only by amassing an ever-increasing amount of money can I keep my family and myself safe.

Primary Emotion:
Fear—Life will crush him.

Secondary Emotions:
Anger—He must take care of himself. There is no one to help. Shame—To be human and vulnerable is shameful; he feels that he must not show his feelings or others will ridicule him.

Money Represents:
A wall of defense in a hostile world

Seeks Comfort by:
Amassing greater amounts of money

Avenues for Growth and Integration:
Seeing that his prison is of his own making; connecting with others; awareness of his vulnerable side; letting himself love and be loved in return

Characteristic Self-Concepts of the Hoarder

Check the statements that feel true for you.
If you check five or more, the Hoarder is your money script.

___ Money is a security blanket.

___ The most important thing one can pass on to one's children is a sufficient amount of money.

___ The worth of a man is judged by the size of the fortune he is able to amass.

___ Money can be used as a bastion against an unpredictable future.

___ Information about money is something to be closely guarded.

___ Money is life's most serious concern.

___ I am willing to be generous with my children if they prove themselves responsible and prudent.

___ The object is not pleasure or power but security.

> The sage does not hoard. Having bestowed all he has on others, he has yet more; having given all he has to others, he is richer still.
>
> ~ Lao-Tzu

The Procrastinator

The Procrastinator has learned that the phrase "cold, hard reality" is only too apt. Doubting his own place in the world and his own capacity to establish one, the Procrastinator takes refuge in rosy-colored, soft-edged fantasies. He will often go to great lengths to avoid having his illusions shattered. The idea of asserting himself in the world in a meaningful way is both foreign and frightening. He feels it is safer to assume a passive, agreeable persona that allows him to slip through the world unnoticed. This makes it possible for the Procrastinator to focus his energy inwardly, maintaining his inner world, where he feels safest.

Core Belief:
I'll deal with it next week.

Primary Emotion:
Fear—It will all come crashing down on him. His procrastination will do him in.

Secondary Emotions:
Anger—He feels that he can never get his head above water financially; he feels anger at others when they force him to look at his avoidance. Shame—He is embarrassed about neglected obligations and about his seeming incapacity to deal with money issues in a timely way.

Money Represents:
Unpleasant reality; the giving up of fantasy in order to deal with reality

Seeks comfort by:
Denial, keeping his head in the sand

Avenues for Growth and Integration:
To begin to really feel and accept the connection between what one does today and what happens tomorrow

Characteristic Self-Concepts of the Procrastinator

Check the statements that feel true for you.
If you check five or more, the Procrastinator is your money script.

___ I know I need to put money aside, but something always seems to interfere.

___ I have all I can do to deal with the present, and the future seems a long way off.

___ I know how to handle money "the right way," but any move to do so makes me too anxious.

___ To really look at my financial situation feels scary, so I put it off.

___ I know that I need to get my financial papers and other affairs in order, but I don't make them a priority.

___ I would like to talk to a financial planning professional at some point, but I'm afraid they would put demands on me that would be too much.

___ I can get scared and angry with myself for my lack of good money management.

___ Sometimes I feel frozen and cannot seem to deal with financial tasks.

> In delay there lies no plenty.
> ~ **William Shakespeare**

The Prince or Princess

The Prince lives in a world without limitations. He can feel unencumbered by financial reality and then feel terrified when he realizes the checking account is overdrawn. Given a sense of specialness and a feeling of unreality about financial limits by his parents, he finds it difficult to acknowledge either necessary limitations on spending or realistic expectations of earning. His task is to come to grips with his almost childlike perception of himself as one who should be provided for, and to accept responsibility for living within his means. An adult sense of responsibility and empowerment can allow him to truly make use of his talents, giving him more solid ground to stand on.

Core Belief:
I am entitled to be provided for.

Primary Emotion:
Anger—The perceived promises of unending support made by the parent or spouse are not as certain as he feels he has been promised. There is a sense of being abandoned or betrayed.

Secondary Emotions:
Fear—The bubble will burst, and the apparent promise of being taken care of will prove to be untrue. Shame—He fails to take responsibility for himself and feels unprepared for the challenges he must face in life.

Money Represents:
The illusions of childhood and the omnipotence of the parent

Seeks Comfort by:
A sense of entitlement

Avenues for Growth and Integration:
Taking responsibility for his own financial well-being; dealing with money issues in a courageous and straightforward manner

Characteristic Self-Concepts of the Prince/Princess

Check the statements that feel true for you.
If you check five or more, the Prince/Princess is your money script.

___ I usually feel there will be plenty for me, so it comes as a shock when there is not.

___ It seems only fair that I should be provided for comfortably.

___ Dealing with the nitty-gritty of money is boring and irritating to me.

___ I sometimes spend as if the sky is the limit and then get scared when faced with my financial limitations.

___ I sometimes make generous gestures and then realize I have overextended myself.

___ The idea of having to plan for the future sometimes feels foreign to me.

___ My parents made me feel I would always be taken care of, and it is quite jarring to find that is not necessarily the case.

___ I wasn't given the tools to understand and deal with money effectively, and I sometimes feel overwhelmed by dealing with money issues.

> The willingness to accept responsibility for one's own life is the source from which self-respect springs.
> ~ Joan Didion,
> Writer

The Gambler

Underneath the Gambler's facade is depression and despair. He cannot psychologically afford to feel these emotions, so he channels his energy into high-risk financial schemes. The riskiness of these schemes serves many functions for him psychologically. There is, of course, the possibility of a big payoff if the scheme succeeds in making money, and there is the rush that goes with that. There is also a rush in the risk itself—putting it all on the line for a gamble. This intensity moves his attention away from his depression and relationships, and serves as a defense against feeling.

Core Belief:

Risk-taking with money is like a drug; I'd rather have the rush of getting it fast than the boredom of careful planning.

Primary Emotion:

Shame—He avoids facing his underlying depression and his addiction to high-risk ventures.

Secondary Emotions:

Fear—He will lose it all after taking an unwise amount of risk. Anger—He will blame himself for losing it all after taking an unwise amount of risk.

Money Represents:

Excitement, a rush

Seeks Comfort by:

Looking for a windfall, a quick fix, or a rush

Avenues for Growth and Integration:

Working with a twelve-step program to bring the addiction under control

Characteristic Self-Concepts of the Gambler

Check the statements that feel true for you.
If you check five or more, the Gambler is your money script.

___ When I take a high risk, I feel excited and alive.

___ I can work with my investments online for hours at a time and not notice the time going by.

___ I sometimes make financial moves that others would consider far too risky.

___ I keep some of my financial dealings hidden from my family.

___ I sometimes cannot wait to get away from people so I can work with my investments.

___ I love the high when my risks pay off.

___ I can get very angry with myself when I lose on a gamble.

___ I sometimes feel more excited about my money gambles than I do about the people in my life.

> You cannot beat a roulette table unless you steal money from it.
> ~ **Albert Einstein**

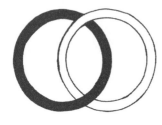

The Co-Dependent

The Co-Dependent seeks to please others in her relationships. Many of this script have grown up in a household focused on an addictive or self-absorbed, demanding parent. The Co-Dependent sets aside her own needs in an effort to please her partner. The partner may or may not be making a mess of things financially, but in either case, the Co-Dependent is more concerned with propping him up than in paying attention to, or actualizing, her own needs.

Core Belief:
I keep the peace by leaving money issues up to my partner.

Primary Emotion:
Fear—Her partner will abandon her if she deals directly with difficult issues.

Secondary Emotions:
Shame—She often feels a deep and generalized sense of humiliation.
Anger—She feels unattended to and invisible.

Money Represents:
A way to appease another and thus ward off abandonment

Seeks Comfort by:
Making herself invisible; meeting the needs of others, often losing herself in the process

Avenues for Growth and Integration:
Supporting her own needs and feelings; setting appropriate boundaries and limits with others

Characteristic Self-Concepts of the Co-Dependent

Check the statements that feel true for you.
If you check five or more, the Co-Dependent is your money script.

___ I usually leave money decisions up to someone else.

___ I don't think of myself where money is concerned; I focus more on the money needs of others.

___ When I feel uncomfortable with the decisions my partner makes, I usually try to smooth things over rather than confronting him.

___ I often feel invisible in my relationships.

___ I often act as if my primary role is to support my partner's money decisions, even though a part of me would like to be more involved.

___ I lack confidence in my ability to make good money decisions.

___ I sometimes feel that I am not worthy of good self-care.

___ I am often ruled by fear where money is concerned.

> The surest way to make ourselves crazy is to get involved in other people's business, and the quickest way to become sane and happy is to tend to our own affairs.
>
> **~ Melody Beattie, Writer**

What If None of the Money Scripts Describe Your Issues?

If it feels to you like none of the money scripts really fit, this section is for you! We invite you to identify the money script that really captures your issues with money. Take some time to ask yourself the following questions:

1. How do you get into difficulty with money?
2. When you look honestly at yourself, how would you describe your money issues?
3. If you could give a name or a title to your money struggles, what would it be?
4. If you were to resolve your emotional issues with money, what would that look like?
5. If there were spiritual lessons for you to learn in dealing with money, what would they be?

> Introjection is the reflexive ingestion of experience. Through it the individual is merged with society.
> ~ Erviny Polster, Psychologist

Understanding your unconscious tendencies with money is the royal road to economic empowerment. No matter what your money script, whether it is one of scripts we have identified or a script that you have fashioned to portray your particular history and issues with money, you gain a great deal by understanding your script. When looked at from a spiritual perspective, your negative money script is a life lesson you carry with you—something you must move past in order to grow in wisdom. When looked at psychologically, the money script represents remnants from your family of origin that, when worked through, enhance your empowerment and self-awareness. When looked at economically, working through the money script provides a framework to keep you from acting unconsciously against your own interests. In all aspects of your economic life, identifying your challenges will help you move beyond them.

Working with Your Money Script

What does it look like to work with your money script? To get a picture of it, let's look at a real-life example.

"John" came to us as a financial planning client with what seemed like a straightforward request: he wanted help making wise investment choices with the $1,000,000 he had just netted on a large real estate transaction. As we worked with an investment plan, John's anxiety level began to rise. It was all he could do to stay seated in his chair. "I just don't think this is going to work," he finally said. "You have good ideas, but I'm getting the feeling that I'd better handle this on my own."

At that point, we realized we were dealing with someone caught in his money script. We began to talk with John about his recent experiences with money. He had been a real estate developer since his early twenties and had been successful in putting together highly lucrative deals. Every time he made a small fortune, however, he quickly lost it. For twenty years he had lived a life of boom followed by bust. In fact, it was with the hope of finally getting off this financial roller-coaster that he had sought out financial consultation.

As we continued to talk, John began to explore his early history with money. Having grown up poor, with an alcoholic father and a depressed mother, John felt a strong fear of poverty—along with a fierce need to protect his family. He still envisioned himself as "the poor kid," even though that was far from his current financial reality. In John's childhood, his father frequently told him that he was worthless and predicted a disastrous future for him. Not surprisingly, John carried negative feelings about himself. He defended himself against these negative feelings by developing an overly aggressive style in his investing and business dealings. This overbearing style, typical of the Power Player, drove him to non-stop deal-making. Because of his need to prove himself to his critical father, he found it nearly impossible to listen to the wisdom of others, or even to access his own internal wisdom. He drove himself to succeed again and again yet was never able to look objectively at his finances. This set him up to repeatedly lose everything he had gained.

> The strongest principle of growth lies in choice.
> ~ George Eliot

> The man who is aware of himself is henceforward independent; and he is never bored, and life is only too short, and he is steeped through and through with a profound yet temperate happiness.
>
> ~ Virginia Woolf

Luckily, John was bright and his exhaustion from the constant rollercoaster ride made him willing to explore the origins of his money script and to experiment with different ways of dealing with money. As he worked with his Money Journal, he began to understand more clearly the connections between the messages he received in childhood and the money script he was playing out. As his understanding and awareness grew, his anxiety lessened. Rather than being ruled by the buried subconscious voices of his past, John became increasingly able to make wise choices about money matters. He put 75 percent of the $1,000,000 into a moderately conservative asset allocation strategy with low-expense ratio funds, as we describe in chapter 10. He did some formal planning for his family, as described in chapter 12. He also purchased some long-overdue life insurance that was needed to fill in gaps for his family in the event of an early death, as discussed in chapter 13. Finally, he put together a tax-smart and family-smart estate plan, as described in chapter 14. The remaining 25 percent of his profits he kept to fund the higher risk real estate ventures in which he specialized.

John is still, and will probably always be, a Power Player. But now he can choose to be a Power Player who recognizes his own strengths and weaknesses, and can balance being a Power Player with prudent financial choices.

John's example shows the power inherent in recognizing and working with your money script. Like John, as you increase your awareness of the messages from your past and the ways they impact you, you will become increasingly able to make life-affirming financial choices. In the next chapter, we will give you the psychological tools you need to transform the negative aspects of your money script into positive, empowering actions that are capable of transforming your financial life.

FROM MONEY SCRIPT TO EMPOWERMENT

5

Your money script is a residue from your past. It defines how you would live out your economic life if you were to live an unexamined life. The very fact that you are reading this book, however, means that you are engaged in the process of examining your financial life. Change starts with understanding where you are. So let's begin our journey into empowerment with an understanding of how you can work with your past.

Your Unique Money Constellation

The set of circumstances you were born into is an existential given in your life. There is no possibility of going back in time to trade in your childhood for another. This simple fact raises many intriguing possibilities. Your childhood creates a set of economic issues for you that you have the opportunity to work through in your adult life. These issues relate to your social class, your ethnic identity, your family's money history, your family's covert rules about money, and your role in the family. Let us consider the idea that this whole set of economic issues, your "money constellation," is the right set of issues for your soul's growth. Say, for example, that a soul comes into this world needing to learn about finding her voice. The set of issues in her money constellation lead her to the money script of the Co-Dependent. She is stuck for years in that role, as her

> You come into the world with a destiny ... there is an individual image that belongs to your soul.
> ~ James Hillman, Psychologist

husband is irresponsible with the family money. One day she goes to the ATM and finds there are no funds in the checking account. This catalyzes a series of events in her relationship and in her consciousness. She begins to look at her history and learns to speak up, set boundaries, and assert herself in her marriage. This entire process turns out to be incredibly important learning for her—at a soul level. She is learning to find her voice. But none of this soul growth would have happened if her childhood had been perfect!

Economic Necessity as a Catalyst to Change

Money issues have a way of making us confront issues in ourselves that we would otherwise have avoided; these are the issues of the Economic Self. Such issues include the need to assert our value in the workplace, marketing our services, asserting ourselves in our relationships, and setting financial limits with our children. All of these diverse issues have in common the fact that we need to stretch beyond our limited self-concept in order to meet our needs. Money issues make us reach beyond our usual limits because the stakes are so high.

Money is absolutely required in modern life! When we reach the point at which we simply cannot ignore our old, unhealthy money patterns, we come face to face with ourselves. Herein lies the gift that money issues bring us: they make us confront old patterns of thinking, behaving, and responding. What greater gift can there be but the opportunity to change and grow?

When the contradictions of the old money script become too great, it's time to change and grow. Sarah is a single woman in her forties who grew up in a lower middle class family. She was worried about having enough money for retirement and came to us for financial consultation. She was right to be concerned. She had not put sufficient resources toward her retirement. Although she is a woman of enor-

> Life's challenges are not supposed to paralyze you, they're supposed to help you discover who you are.
> ~ Bernice Johnson Reagon, Musician

mous professional talent, she had a limited self-concept and had avoided taking on leadership roles at work. Now the money issues in her life were forcing her to make changes in her work life. She resolved to take on new projects at work, joined several committees at her workplace, and performed her work with new passion. After six months of this, she discussed a raise with her boss, which he gave her quite readily. Taking on leadership roles, taking on new responsibilities, and letting herself be in the limelight at work were all important steps for her to take, and she would have confronted none of them had it not been for economic necessity.

From Feeling to Action

One of the key ingredients of emotional intelligence is the ability to tie what you feel to your choices. There is a cycle of experience that starts with feeling and leads to insight and action. For example, Joanne felt guilty about the fact that she did not care for her financial advisor, who was chosen by her father. When her father died, Joanne came into a sizable inheritance. The money came with her father's advisor, a condescending man who never took Joanne seriously. It had been Joanne's way in the past to discount her own feelings and interpret any negative feeling as a failing on her part. Working with her money script, Joanne found that she was the Princess. She had no experience in questioning the decisions of the king, her father. She came to realize that her negative feelings about her financial advisor were quite justified. Her feelings were in fact an emotional intelligence, signaling to her that she needed to make a change. She found a new advisor who supported her both emotionally and financially. It was in learning to listen to her feelings that Joanne found that she needed to take action.

> A little knowledge that acts is worth infinitely more than much knowledge that is idle.
> ~ Kahlil Gibran, Poet

Recognizing the Feelings

Feelings about money issues are difficult to distinguish at first because these feelings are so tied up with feelings left over from childhood. As you work with this book, you will understand your money script from childhood, and you will gain a new perspective on your old feelings. This new perspective allows you to understand what you feel and distinguishes helpful feelings from old Superego Attacks, which simply make you feel bad about yourself. As we discussed in chapter 1, a Superego Attack is an internal voice that beats up on you and berates you for your feelings. Suppose you are feeling angry and hurt that you aren't being sufficiently rewarded for the work you do; you feel that you really should be making more money at your job. As you start to feel these perhaps very legitimate feelings, your Superego Attack says, "You are not worth a penny more than they are paying you. If you ask for more, they will just laugh in your face." You come to recognize the Superego Attack for what it is—a cruel left-over from childhood. In recognizing the Superego Attack, you are able to set aside its harsh judgment and can mobilize your energy to negotiate for that long-deserved raise.

Learn to recognize the feelings that are alive inside of you, for those feelings are the spark of your own emotional intelligence, guiding you toward economic growth and empowerment. You will notice that deeper, more creative feelings come with a sense of openness and vulnerability, whereas the Superego Attack feels harsh, judgmental, and invulnerable. Creative, life-affirming states of consciousness are always more vulnerable, open spaces than the closed down, harsh stance of the inner critic. Money is often associated with this harsher, more critical and competitive frame of mind, but the pathway to true prosperity is characterized by creativity, openness, and a willingness to risk.

Perhaps it is a product of our patriarchal heritage that causes many of us to associate financial empowerment with a kind of hardness of spirit. We think of financial "tough guys" like Donald Trump, whose trademark phrase is "You're fired!" We think of the hardened faces of CEOs in expensive suits that are worn like coats of armor. But there are many

Our life is composed greatly from dreams, from the unconscious, and they must be brought into connection with action. They must be woven together.

~ Anaïs Nin, Writer

roads that lead to Rome. Your path to financial empowerment need not look like anybody's but your own. Isn't it a
relief to know that you don't have to be like Donald Trump
or Martha Stewart to find your pathway to prosperity? Finding your own true and empowered voice in this world is a
process of unfoldment that brings you into a new relationship with money. This is your journey. You don't have to live
it by archaic, patriarchal rules that diminish your creativity
and shut down your sense of connection to others.

In the spirit of creativity and vulnerability, you must
develop a positive, nurturing relationship with the fantasies
and imagery in your mind. It is this imagery that can help
you find the dreams you wish to actualize. Consider Sally,
who had a harsh Superego and had never expressed the
imagery that lay right below the surface. In consultation she
had an image of herself as the goddess Aphrodite with flowing hair—glowing with sexual vitality and beauty. Taking
great pleasure in having her inner imagery heard and
delighted in, she began to connect the image with her
dreams in life. In her Economic Self, she had been living
out the money script of the Coupon Clipper, forsaking any
pleasure that money could buy her and instead saving every
penny despite her sizable net-worth. As she connected with
the image of herself as the beautiful Aphrodite, she found
new energy. She shared that she had always wanted to go to
Europe with her husband but had considered it "wasteful"
to spend money on travel. New vistas opened up for Sally,
and she gave herself the permission to travel. Not only did
she end up loving it, but sharing her dream with her husband also breathed new life into her marriage.

> I celebrate myself and sing myself.
> ~ Walt Whitman

Mobilizing Your Energy

Once you get clear about your money feelings and images,
you can focus on mobilizing energy to meet the world with
new self-assertion. Edward, for example, had deep-seated
grief. His father had died a year earlier and left him his

childhood home. Edward was the sole executor of his father's estate. It was clear to everyone in his family—including Edward—that he needed to sell the house, but he could not bring himself to do what he needed to do. As Edward became more aware of the grief he was feeling for his father, he allowed himself to cry and express his grief. In doing so, he found that his energy for selling the house started to form. He was allowing himself to grieve both the loss of his father and the loss of the home he had lived in as a child. Now he was ready to let go and no longer needed to take care of himself by procrastinating about his duties as his father's executor.

Exercise: Imagining an Abundant, Powerful You— A Guided Meditation

Turn down any music and the phones—create a peaceful environment. Let your body relax. We are going to take a journey into the imagery that lies deep inside your consciousness. Breathe deeply. With the inhale, your mantra is "I am always connected." With the exhale, your mantra is "Spirit guides my path." Let yourself relax into this truth. Breathing deeply and fully, stay with this mantra for a time—until you feel a deep sense of relaxation in your mind and body.

Imagine that you live in a world of total abundance. Poverty does not exist in this fantasy. You are totally free. There are no economic constraints. Your prosperity takes nothing away from any other person in this fantasy. Your fullness helps the world itself to become more full. How does it feel in your body to be free like this? You are free of greed and fear in this fantasy. There is abundance for you—abundance for all.

Enter deeply into this fantasy. You are feeling free, abundant, unburdened, beautiful, and powerful.

Now, consider the imagery in your mind. How do you see yourself in this state of freedom? Where are you? How do you feel? How do you look? What are you wearing? Who is around you? As you get ready to return to the room and to everyday consciousness, know that this image of yourself as beautiful, abundant, and powerful is yours to keep. Take it in fully. Pay attention to the details of your imagery; this will help you

> Emotional intelligence is the ability to sense, understand, and effectively apply the power and acumen of emotions as a source of human energy, information, connection, and influence.
> ~ Robert K. Cooper,
>   Leadership Consultant

remember. Now let yourself return to the room, but hold on to this imagery. You can come back to it any time you wish.

Feelings Inform Action

Your feelings inform your action. Once you really feel and express what is happening inside of you, there is a natural flow to new energy. When you start to feel this new energy, it is important to recognize it and let it invigorate movement inside you. When Edward started to feel his new energy around his executor duties, he called a real estate agent to put the house on the market. Maybe it was just good luck or maybe it was synchronicity, but that same day a close friend from work told him that he was looking for a house. His friend ended up buying the house at market value, and Edward got an extra gift: he now visits his friend a few times a year and enjoys being in his old house with all the memories it still holds for him.

There is an ancient Sufi saying: "Man takes one step forward and a hundred angels clear his path." There is magic in mobilizing your energy. When you start to actualize your financial goals, good energy seems to lead to more good energy.

Taking Informed Action

You are getting more in tune with your feelings. You are feeling new energy. Now it is time to take action. In the world of money, taking action is no simple task. If you take the wrong action, you could do yourself more harm than good.

When it comes to investing, you need to be realistic about what you know and what you do not know. Another hitch with diving into the investing world is that there are all too many sharks swimming in the waters. It is imperative that you either learn investing basics yourself or find a competent and ethical advisor to guide you. In many cases, doing both will serve you best.

Our intuition and feelings guide us in our interpersonal lives, but when it comes to investing we need to be

> Go confidently in the direction of your dreams. Live the life you have imagined.
> ~ **Henry David Thoreau**

informed and learn its rules. You may be impressed with a company and want to buy its stock, but the company's health and its stock price might be affected by factors that are utterly out of your awareness, such as political instability in the country where it buys its raw materials.

Many aspects of proper investing are counterintuitive like this. For example, it is sometimes important to sell off some of the very portion of your stock portfolio that has done best in the last period. Other times the stock of a company facing difficulty can be a better investment than the stock of a world-class company. Yet another example: When interest rates go up, bond prices go down. Welcome to the strange and counter-intuitive world of investing! True wealth requires more than intuition and common sense. Informed action is key.

> There is nothing so practical as a good theory.
> ~ Kurt Lewin, Social Psychologist

Money Is a Macro Reality

Different principals apply to different scale problems. For example, in physics, if we zoom way in to existence at the micro level of an atom, gravity has virtually no effect. Zoom way, way out to existence at the macro level of a galaxy, and gravity is the great eternal force that holds the stars together. At the personal level, we individuals are (hopefully) guided by our ethics and sense of justice, yet large groups of people (such as corporations) are not governed by a personal sense of right and wrong. A group of people cannot feel the way individuals can; law must instead do for corporations what conscience does for individuals.

Different rules apply at different scales, and so it is with our feelings, intuition, and investing. Feelings and intuition are our best guides in the familiar interpersonal world that we mostly live in. Working with our feelings and intuition brings us toward financial action. Once we start the process of investing, however, we have to orient ourselves to the scale on which money works. It is a large-scale playing field that is more complex than any one human being—no matter how brilliant or intuitive—can totally comprehend.

Money is affected by many, many factors. Here are a few of the almost infinite factors money responds to:

- weather
- the world political climate
- war and peace
- interest rates
- industrial productivity
- world leadership
- disease
- agricultural productivity
- environmental conditions

This list could go on for hundreds of pages. The point is this: Money works at a macro level, and as we have seen, things that work at the macro level follow different rules than things that work at the micro level. Therefore, sound investing calls for an appreciation of its rules. You don't need to be a pilot to take a flight on a 747, but you do need to let the pilot fly the plane. So it is with investing: You don't have to be a Wall Street analyst to make sound investment choices, but you are much better off if you either learn the theory of investing or listen to those who understand it.

In chapters 10 through 16 we will cover the Six Pillars of Your Financial Success.

1. Smart Investing
2. Home Ownership
3. Empowered Earning
4. Conscious Spending and Credit
5. Adequate Insurance
6. Wise Planning

Each of the six pillars involves understanding the road rules of that particular dimension. Earning and spending,

> An increase of a few powers of ten results in qualitative change . . . in short, more is different.
> ~ **Joel R. Primack, Physicist**

for instance, are areas where your intuition and feelings are powerful guides to economic empowerment. Investing, on the other hand, can be quite counterintuitive, especially for the beginner. Insurance is also an area where understanding its principles can lead to economically rewarding results. Estate planning involves primarily tax law and follows its own principles and precedents.

Economic empowerment calls on us to let others into our decision-making process so we can make well-informed choices. As we have said from the start, money is the ultimate interpersonal issue: we can't earn it all alone, and in order to work with it wisely, we need to reach out to others who understand the principles of investing.

Being Curious, Vulnerable, and Open to Help

One pitfall some people fall into is that they skip over the vulnerability they feel in learning about money. It takes courage to admit that you don't know something; it takes getting past pride. The problem is, of course, that if you don't acknowledge the feeling of vulnerability that goes with learning new financial skills, you will never open up the space in yourself to learn. This goes also for allowing a financial planner to help you. And there is vulnerability involved in working with a financial planner, as it is hard to choose one. What if he or she is a crook or is incompetent?

It can be difficult to let another person into an area of your life that you are not fully comfortable with yourself. Yet if you don't learn about money and let yourself receive professional financial advice, you may be setting yourself up to make basic investing mistakes. Later in the book we will cover investing basics and give you tips to help you find a qualified financial planner. For now, let us say that it is a good thing be curious about how money works, to acknowledge what you don't yet know about money, and to be open to sound professional advice.

> Advances are made by answering questions. Discoveries are made by questioning answers.
> ~ Bernhard Haisch, Astrophysicist

Your Roadmap to Financial Empowerment

In this chapter, we have provided you a roadmap for finding your financial empowerment. Once you get in touch with your past and become aware of your money script, you begin the process of change. New choices begin to open up for you. The next factor in making change is mobilizing your energy. You take your newly found feelings and choices about how you want to show up in the world as an economic actor, and you move into action. Once you act, you must be willing to act in an informed way. Money has its own rules— it does not act according to any one person's feelings or intuition—because it reflects a macro and collective reality. It is best that you acquaint yourself with money basics and find an informed advisor who can help you take wise financial action.

> When we were children, we used to think that when we were grown up we would no longer be vulnerable. But to grow up is to accept vulnerability.... To be alive is to be vulnerable.
> **~ Madeleine L'Engle, Writer**

With these powerful tools, you can change the economic landscape of your life. What's more, the changes you make can be hugely energizing and can help you express the fullness of who you really are at the deepest level. As you come fully into your Economic Self, you will discover confidence that will give new vitality to you in all aspects of your being.

LOVE AND MONEY

6

My (Daisy's) mother grew up during the Depression and carried a sense of scarcity—along with a great deal of anxiety about money—throughout her life. One of her oft-repeated sayings was, "When the wolf comes in the door, love goes out the window." It's true that maintaining a loving relationship in the midst of financial difficulties is challenging. What is impossible, however, is maintaining a loving relationship when there is distrust, resentment, power imbalances, or lack of communication about money. Statistically, money and sex are the two leading causes of marital unhappiness and divorce.

As the Beatles told us in the sixties, "Money can't buy me love." In this chapter we're going to look at how to combine love AND money. Whether you're in a committed relationship, dating a "significant other," or single, learning to communicate clearly and lovingly about financial matters is a vital piece of developing a healthy Economic Self.

To successfully combine love and money, you must understand and honor five principles:

- Generosity
- Empathy
- Transparency
- Trust
- Respect for Boundaries

> Someone to tell it to is one of the fundamental needs of human beings.
> ~ Miles Franklin, Writer

Generosity

This is the primary principle—the foundation on which all the others rest. Webster offers several definitions for generosity: (1) willingness to give, (2) nobility of thought or behavior, and (3) abundance. When you experience loving feelings toward someone, you have a willingness to give. Generosity comes naturally, without question or strain. I remember the early days with my high school boyfriend. We celebrated weekly anniversaries. I never went into a store without looking for some token that would remind him of my tender feelings for him. Sweet, though they are, these early days of courtship inevitably give way to a more prosaic "starting to take each other for granted" period. It is at this point that the second definition, "nobility of thought or behavior," becomes vitally important.

Acting lovingly, even when we may feel anything but loving, is especially important when times get tough. A friend told me a lovely story about the early days of her marriage. She and her husband were both graduate students, pinching every penny to manage on a limited budget. The only luxury she allowed herself was a cappuccino on her way to work each morning. During one of their weekly financial powwows, where they juggled the bills and tried to make their checkbook balance, it became clear that the cappuccino would need to go. "That's OK. I'll just get one on Sundays," she told her husband. The next morning she found a $20 bill tucked into her purse with a note that read: "For my lovely wife. I can't give you much right now, but I can afford to buy your cappuccinos." My friend never was sure exactly where her husband got the money. She suspects that he must have gone without a number of lunches.

Looking back on the experience she said, "Jerry was able to make me feel rich in spite of the little money we had. I knew that with him my life would be full of surprising rewards no matter what our financial situation was." Twenty years later, she has been proven right. Her husband's gen-

> Since you get more joy out of giving joy to others, you should put a good deal of thought into the happiness that you are able to give.
> ~ Eleanor Roosevelt

erosity of spirit has helped the two of them maintain a loving connection through the inevitable challenges of life. Moreover, the feeling of being rich has supported them in actually manifesting abundance in their lives.

Exercise: Written Meditation

You can do this exercise on your own; or if you have a willing partner, do this exercise simultaneously and then compare notes. In your Money Journal, begin a "written meditation" on the following questions. To do this, allow yourself to sit for a few moments with the question. Then, without planning, begin to write. See if you can write without stopping for five to ten minutes. Try not to censor yourself. It doesn't matter whether your writing makes sense to anyone else. The objective is to give yourself an opportunity to explore and perhaps make some discoveries about yourself.

> Kindess in words creates confidence. Kindness in thinking creates profoundness. Kindness in giving creates love.
>
> ~ Lao-Tzu

1. When have I been on the receiving end of a generous gesture? (This may have been from a partner, parent, or other significant person—maybe even a stranger.)
2. What impact did this gesture have on me? How did I feel? Did it result in a change in my behavior? Did it change the way I viewed myself?
3. When have I been the one to offer a generous gesture?
4. How did being the giver affect me?
5. What impact did it have on the receiver?
6. How was the relationship affected?

When you feel ready, share the results of your meditation with your partner. You may want to actually read what you have written or simply use it as a basis to begin a conversation.

Empathy

To truly experience empathy for your partner requires two things: setting your own feelings/wishes aside for the moment and opening your heart to truly hear and resonate with what your partner is telling you. To do these things can stir up many complicated emotions. You may feel frightened at your own vulnerability. You may feel resentment at attending to another's needs when you have pressing needs of your own. You may feel a sense of competition with your partner. ("My feelings are more correct or more significant. You should listen to me.") All these emotions are valid and understandable. As we discussed in the previous section, however, to nurture an intimate relationship you must be willing to act lovingly—sometimes despite your own feelings. Of course, no one wants a one-sided relationship. Your empathy for your partner must be matched by his or her willingness to empathize with you. If, over time, you find that this is not the case, you will want to seek out professional couples counseling and/or reconsider the relationship. Assuming that both of you are willing to take the risk of experiencing and expressing empathy for the other, here is an exercise designed to foster that empathy.

> The more I give to thee,
> the more I have, for both are
> infinite. Take my breath away.
> ~ **William Shakespeare**

Exercise: Listening with Empathy

Find a comfortable, private space to talk, and sit facing your partner. You will both have the opportunity to be the speaker and the listener, so decide who will speak first. Then proceed with the following steps.

- The speaker will talk for two to three minutes about an issue that is significant to the relationship and about which there is disagreement.
- When the speaker is finished, the listener will echo back what he or she heard the speaker saying. It's not necessary to repeat the exact words; the objective is to accurately reflect the speaker's feelings.
- The speaker will then agree that the listener has "gotten it" or ask the listener to make adjustments until the reflection feels right.
- The listener will then say something like: "I can understand how you would feel that way. It must be scary to have me suggest looking for a new car when we don't have the credit cards paid off yet."
- Now switch roles and repeat the steps.
- When you have completed the exercise, set the issue aside at least until the next day. Give yourselves time to integrate the impact of resonating with your partner's feelings and having your partner respond empathetically to yours.

This may be a difficult exercise to do at first. You will probably want to begin by discussing issues that are less emotionally loaded and move gradually into more challenging areas. Remember that you and your partner are exploring new territory. Be patient with yourselves. Don't forget to appreciate each other for the courage you're showing in deepening your relationship. Don't wait until you have it "perfect" before you celebrate yourselves!

Transparency

We all have a longing to be truly known by another. At the same time, the thought of being really "seen" in our entirety can stir up a great deal of anxiety. "If anyone were to see who I really am, they would (judge, reject, abandon) me." Because of thoughts like this, many of us spend a great deal of energy in an effort to show only the parts of ourselves that we deem acceptable. Sometimes we mange to conceal some parts even from ourselves. If we want to become spiritually mature human beings, however—if we want intimacy in our lives—we must be willing to explore all of ourselves.

As Carl Jung says, "We do not become enlightened by visualizing beings of light, but by making the darkness conscious." The more we become comfortable with ourselves, the more willing we will be to share all aspects of ourselves with our partners: "When I allow you to see my weaknesses and vulnerabilities, I increase the likelihood of you being able to empathize with me. When I help you to understand me, the chances are much greater that you will feel trusting and open to me."

There are two aspects to transparency. One involves being open about your history. You have learned a great deal in the earlier chapters of this book about yourself and your family of origin. It's important to share what you have learned with your partner. As your understanding of yourself develops further, it will be important to keep your partner abreast of your discoveries. It's also important to be open to insights that your partner may offer about you.

> The saddest part about being human is not paying attention. Presence is the gift of life.
> ~ Stephen Levine, Poet

The second aspect of transparency is expressing your thoughts and feelings authentically in the moment. It's especially useful if you can connect your current thoughts and feelings to your history: "I find myself getting really anxious when you talk about wanting a new car. I know that you know we can't afford one right now. I remember that never stopped my dad, though. If he talked about wanting something today, you could bet that tomorrow it would appear. My mother was constantly ducking creditors, and once we even had the phone cut off because my dad had spent the money on some fancy toy for himself." Being transparent in this way allows your partner to empathize with your feelings rather than feeling attacked and defensive.

When working with the principle of transparency, though, we have one important caution. Before you share a feeling—especially if it is a feeling about your partner—stop and think: Can I share this feeling in a way that will move the relationship forward rather than set it back? If I'm angry, can I simply give voice to my anger without accusing or berating? If I need to tell you something difficult to hear, can I wait for an appropriate time rather than blurting it out when you are already sad or upset?

> You should take a chance with the truth. The truth is always worth it.
> ~ Anonymous

Exercise: Representing Yourself

This exercise has two parts. The first part you will do on your own. Once you have completed this part, you can decide when or whether you wish to do the second part with your partner.

Part 1: Open your Money Journal in such a way that there are two clean pages facing each other. On the left hand page will be a representation of the Self that you present to the world. This could be a realistic figure or something very abstract. You might even want to make a collage out of photos, pictures from magazines, and so on. On the facing page will be a representation of the Self that you keep concealed. Again, this can take whatever form you wish. When the two pages are complete (at least for the moment), contemplate the representations and what they mean to you. Do you have an emotional reaction to the work you've done?

Part 2: Consider how much, if any, of your work you'd like to share with your partner. Don't push yourself to reveal more than you're ready to. This is a process of self-discovery and you must reach a certain comfort level with yourself before you're ready to share your discovery with another.

Trust

If there is mutual generosity, empathy, and transparency between you and your partner, there will almost inevitably be trust. Trust means believing that your partner has your best interests at heart; it means feeling secure that your partner has "got your back." Virginia Satir once said, "Real love does not mean holding hands and gazing eternally into each other's eyes. Rather, it means holding hands and gazing outward in the same direction." Do you trust your partner to be gazing in the same direction you are? Do you share goals, priorities, and hopes for the future?

> The meeting of two personalities is like the contact of two chemical substances: if there is any reaction, both are transformed.
> **~ Carl Jung, Founder of Analytical Psychology**

Exercise: Week with $100

This exercise, based on a suggestion by Suze Orman, is especially useful for couples who are not yet formally committed or who have not co-mingled their bank accounts. Even for long-time married couples, however, it can provide some valuable insights.

- At the beginning of the week, you will give your partner $100 in cash. He or she will do the same for you.
- For the coming week, you will each be responsible for spending the other's money.
- Once the week is over, compare notes. How did each of you spend the money? Does either of you have any left over? How did it feel to be spending your partner's money? What are your feelings about the ways your partner spent your money?

Building trust

To give you some ideas about the possibilities of this exercise, consider Sam and Elizabeth's experience. As a newly engaged couple, they had discussed many issues. But the topic of money stirred up a lot of anxiety for both of them, and they had done their best to avoid it. When they came to see us for financial planning, we suggested that they try this exercise before doing anything else. We felt sure that it would give them a better understanding of their own and each other's approach to money than would many hours of simply discussing financial details.

Sam and Elizabeth both took the exercise seriously. They wanted to spend the money in ways that would be pleasing to the other and demonstrate their commitment to the relationship. Interestingly, however, they went about this in very different ways. Sam focused on being generous to Elizabeth. He looked on the $100 as "found money" and used it for luxuries and little surprises. He brought her flowers, took her out to an elegant brunch, and managed to spend the entire sum by Wednesday. Elizabeth, on the other hand, took the money to the local furniture store and used it as a down payment on a sofa she and Sam had both seen as perfect for their new apartment.

When Elizabeth and Sam returned to our office the following week, neither one was happy. Though Elizabeth had enjoyed the treats Sam provided, she felt concerned that he had spent the money "frivolously." She was convinced that this did not bode at all well for establishing a solid financial foundation. Sam was, not surprisingly, disappointed that his generosity wasn't more appreciated. "Doesn't she get that I just wanted to make her happy?" he asked plaintively. Elizabeth's choice of spending the money on furniture (for an apartment they wouldn't move into for several months) seemed "stodgy" and overly conservative to him. He worried that pooling their money would leave him facing a life devoid of the little surprises he so loved.

For this couple to move toward a relationship of trust, it was necessary for each to understand the other. Elizabeth's money script was the Coupon Clipper. She had grown up

> Because we're different, we can have the fun of exchanging worlds, giving our loves and excitements to each other. You can learn music, I can learn flying. And that's only the beginning. I think it would go on for us as long as we live.
> ~ Richard Bach, Writer

with parents who never had quite enough to make ends meet. She longed for financial security and focused on managing her money wisely. If given a choice, she would always opt for the most conservative, cost-effective option. Sam's money script was the Prince. Though he had been raised by a single mother on a limited income, his mother had done everything in her power to make her "baby" feel well-taken care of. She had gone into debt to pay his college tuition, and he had never held a job until after graduation. His unconscious assumption was that he would always be provided for and that he was entitled to the best life had to offer.

Sam and Elizabeth are an example of a couple whose contrasting money scripts led to each feeling misunderstood and unappreciated by the other. They were surprised to learn that the differences between them could actually work to the advantage of the relationship. Once they began to share with each other some of their family history around money, each of them became more understanding and sympathetic toward the other. Sam expressed feelings of great tenderness for Elizabeth's struggles growing up and her anxiety about money in the present. Elizabeth was able to recognize that Sam's mother had unintentionally deprived him of a reality-based understanding of money.

After some hours of talking—both in and out of our office—Sam and Elizabeth came to an agreement: they would set aside a specific amount of money each month for saving and investing. Elizabeth would take charge of ensuring that this sum went into their investment account at the beginning of the month. At the end of the month, money that remained after the bills were paid could be used to treat themselves. Sam would be in charge of coming up with fun, creative ways to spend this "treat" money. Having decided this, both of them were able to relax. The needs of each were being respected and tended. Interestingly, after a couple of years together, Sam and Elizabeth have each moved closer to the center. Elizabeth is much better able to

> Marriage, ultimately, is the practice of becoming passionate friends.
> ~ **Harville Hendrix, Psychotherapist**

enjoy spending money since she knows she can trust Sam to cooperate with her on creating a secure future for their family. For his part, Sam has gotten interested in building their portfolio and will sometimes even suggest that the "treat" money be put toward boosting their IRAs.

Through practicing empathy and transparency with each other, Sam and Elizabeth have built a foundation of trust. This allows them to willingly practice generosity in their relationship.

Respect for Boundaries

The fifth principle is the one that underlies and supports the other four. There are two equally important aspects to this principle: respect for the boundaries of your partner and respect for your own boundaries. We will explore financial boundaries in more detail in chapter 8; here we will look at the financial boundary issues that arise with life partners.

Most of us are familiar with the idea of respecting the boundaries of others. From the time you were a small child you probably heard your parents say things like: "Don't grab the doll—that belongs to your sister" or "Remember to leave some pie for Dad. He's coming home late." Learning to respect our own boundaries is sometimes more difficult. Indeed, we may not really develop an understanding of this principle until well into adulthood.

How well we deal with boundaries around money is largely dependent on our money script. If you have a Co-Dependent or a Power Player script, for instance, you might find yourself struggling to respect others' boundaries. The Co-Dependent rushes in to help or "rescue" the other, which often results in a failure to acknowledge the other's autonomy. The Power Player tends to feel that "I know best and must stay in control." This can lead him to override the other's wishes and stifle his partner's independence.

On the other hand, some money scripts—like that of the Victim—lead to a lack of respect for one's own boundaries.

> Boundaries make living clear and conscious.
>
> ~ Joseph C. Zinker, PhD, Psychologist

If you find yourself often feeling taken advantage of, unfairly treated, or as if your voice is not being heard, you need to pay attention to developing a stronger sense of where your own boundaries lie.

Jeff and Marian are an example of a couple whose money scripts intersected in ways that made it tough for them to respect the fifth principle. Jeff was a well-intentioned but somewhat oblivious Power Player. His parents had pressured him since early adolescence to "make something" of himself, and as they became elderly, they relied more and more on his financial advice and generosity to maintain their lifestyle.

Over the years, Jeff had become convinced that the burden of sustaining the family financially was his alone to carry. He found it almost impossible to listen to anyone else's suggestions or to respect any opinion that differed from his own. Marian's script was that of the Princess. Growing up an only child with older, successful parents, she had developed a "whim of iron." Whatever Marian wanted Marian was accustomed to getting. Jeff took care of her in fine style and required nothing from her in terms of their finances. As long as she maintained a beautiful home and cared for their children, he would handle the money and make all financial decisions.

In many ways, this arrangement suited both Jeff and Marian. They were both comfortable in their established roles and both found their lives together to be quite satisfying. At age forty-five, however, Marian began individual therapy. Her children were nearly grown and she found herself with a vague sense of unease. Her life, which had been so pleasant, now began to feel a little stifling. As Marian worked with her therapist, she began to understand the extent to which she had abdicated her own power in her marriage. Rather than being Jeff's equal partner, she had, in many ways, remained a child. Her initial reaction to this new understanding was rage: "How dare he have kept me in a 'gilded cage' all these years!"

> Men are taught to apologize for their weaknesses, women for their strengths.
> ~ Lois Wyse, Writer

Gradually, however, she began to understand her own part in the family drama. There had been a lot of incentive for her to avoid developing any financial boundaries for herself. After all, being a Princess can be fun—especially if there's a white knight tending to your every wish! After much self-examination, Marian felt ready to open a discussion with Jeff. His first reaction, just like Marian's, was one of anger: "How can you be so ungrateful? I've given you every luxury and you still aren't satisfied!" After several months of tension and distress, Jeff and Marian showed up in our office for some couples work around money. Because they had a lot of love for each other despite their anger, they were willing to look at how they had co-created a relationship in which the financial boundaries ranged from fuzzy to nonexistent. They began to work consciously together toward establishing a marriage between two adults—each with his and her own thoughts, feelings, strengths, and fallibilities.

When the two had been in counseling for about six months, Marian decided to go back to graduate school in order to re-establish her career as a designer. Rather than assuming that Jeff would foot the bills, she worked out a loan agreement with him in which he would pay her tuition and she would begin to repay him as soon as she started working. She felt incredibly empowered with this arrangement and Jeff, much to his surprise, felt liberated. "If I don't have to be in charge of taking care of everyone all the time, maybe I'll have the energy (and extra money) to do what I've always wanted to do." Sure enough, Jeff took a six-month sabbatical from his work and set off on a backpacking trip through Asia. By the time he returned, Jeff and Marian found themselves in a very different relationship. Jeff had an increased willingness to respect Marian's boundaries—she opened a separate checking account for the first time—and Marian had a new respect for her own capacity to be self-supporting.

By empowering herself financially, she set both herself and Jeff free to be equal partners who stayed together out of choice rather than out of need. When we last heard from this couple, Marian had bought a lake house out of her earnings and Jeff—looking at last to his own needs—was considering partial retirement to allow for more travel adventures.

Exercise: Financial Boundaries

Either alone or with your partner, spend some time thinking about your own financial boundaries. Are your boundary difficulties more around respecting your own boundaries or those of the other? What are some of the pay-offs for keeping boundaries murky? What do you know about your parents' struggles with boundaries? How did these struggles affect you during your growing-up years?

Before we leave the issue of boundaries, it's important to consider the flip side of murky boundaries: boundaries that are overly rigid and impermeable. If, for example, you and your partner maintain totally separate financial lives, you might want to consider what effect that has on your intimacy. The goal of establishing clear boundaries is to support a relationship with both intimacy and autonomy.

Take some time to reflect with your partner on the balance of intimacy and autonomy in your relationship. If the relationship seems to veer in one direction or the other, how might you improve the balance?

> Marriage is our last, best chance to grow up.
> ~ Joseph Barth, Theologian

Financial Dimensions of Marriage

Now that we've laid the emotional groundwork, let's look at a more concrete aspect: the financial dimensions of marriage.

Marriage can have a positive effect on your financial well-being. With the splitting of family responsibilities between two adults, marriage has significant personal and financial advantages. Society has encoded many of these advantages into tax and social policies. Here are some of the ways to take financial advantage of being married:

1. If you are both employed, check for double coverage of health, dental, supplemental life insurance plans, and so on. Go with the plan that offers the best coverage for both spouses and opt out of double coverage.

Most employers will reimburse you for coverage you have declined.

2. Again, if you are both employed, check both your 401(k) plans for employer matching. You can use joint funds to maximize any 401(k) matching available to you.

3. Insurance is another area where there may be significant savings for married people. Car, homeowners, and long-term care insurances are areas in which married people are frequently eligible for discounts.

4. One great advantage to being married is that, through the Unlimited Marital Deduction, you can pass your estate on to your spouse without incurring estate taxes. (Your spouse must be an American citizen.) The estate taxes are incurred when your spouse dies, so it is important to consult your financial advisor and an estate-planning attorney about proper use of this deduction.

> Many marriages would be better if the husband and wife clearly understood that they're on the same side.
> ~ Zig Ziglar, Writer

Perhaps the greatest advantage to being married or in a committed relationship, wherein economic resources are shared, is the potential to bring two people's productivity to bear on creating an economically empowered household. In other words, both partners can contribute to making the household thrive. The most obvious example of this is combining two partners' incomes to qualify for buying a home. As we will see in chapter 12, "Building Home Equity," home ownership is a cornerstone of economic success, and combining the resources of two people can make home ownership a reality for many who could not manage it on their own.

Considering Marriage or a Domestic Partnership

When you are getting married or combining financial resources as domestic partners, it is important to take some time to discuss your financial attitudes and realities. Talk with each other about how money was dealt with in your family of origin. Talk with each other about your spending and saving habits. Take some time to go over your investments and debts with each other. Pull out your various banking statements and look at where you both stand financially; it is much better to get the financial issues on the table right from the start.

Open communication is the key to an economically successful marriage or domestic partnership. You don't need to agree on every aspect of your financial lives, but you will be much better off if you can talk about your areas of agreement and disagreement.

Below is an eight-step checklist for combining your financial resources in marriage or domestic partnership:

> The real act of marriage takes place in the heart, not in the ballroom or church or synagogue. It's a choice you make—not just on your wedding day, but over and over again.
> ~ **Barbara de Angelis, Psychologist, Writer**

1. Look over your insurance coverage. Do you have a too little, too much, or duplication in your coverage?
2. Change the beneficiary on your retirement accounts and life insurance. Should anything happen to you, make sure your assets are going to whom you want to leave them.
3. Review any credit card debt with each other. Develop a plan to eliminate credit card debt (see chapter 15, "Credit and Debt Issues," for guidelines on how to approach this).
4. Discuss all additional debts—student loans, personal loans, auto loans, and so on. Getting this information out on the table is the first step to developing an effective debt-elimination plan.
5. Go over your assets. Look at each others' retirement, investment, and bank accounts, and discuss your approach to investing. Is one of you more risk averse than the other?
6. Discuss your families of origin. What was their economic status when you were growing up? What is it now? Was money talked about in your family? Do you have an expectation that you will inherit money

from your family? Do you have an expectation that you will need to support someone from your family?

7. Once you have put all of your assets and debts on the table, you should be able to work up a combined net worth statement—your assets minus your debts. This will give you a good starting place. From here you can set goals to increase your net worth—both by building assets and reducing debt.

8. Develop a budget. It need not be a "to the penny" financial straightjacket, but it can be helpful to set spending goals.

Finding a loving partner with whom you can build a satisfying life is a blessing—but it still requires a great deal of work and cooperation. Some people would insist that one must rely on God or Karma to provide the relationship they want. When we hear people suggest this, we're reminded of an old joke: The city dweller said to the farmer as they looked out over the fields of ripe corn, "God has really blessed you. Just look at all that He's provided." "That's true," replied the farmer, "but you should have seen those fields twenty years ago when God had them all to Himself!"

God provides many blessings, but it is up to you to do the work that allows the blessings to manifest. Establishing and maintaining the relationship you want—romantically and financially—is a lifelong task. The good news is that it is truly a labor of love.

> This is what marriage really means: helping one another to reach the full status of being persons, responsible beings who do not run away from life.
> ~ Paul Tournier,
>   Physician

LIVING HAPPILY *AFTER* "HAPPILY EVER AFTER"

7

It **happens to** the best of us. Sometimes, despite all good intentions, honest efforts, and high hopes, you find yourself in the midst of a divorce or separation. Under the best of circumstances, this is a difficult and painful process. Believe it or not, however, it is possible for you to emerge from it stronger, wiser, and maybe even happier than you would have imagined. In this chapter we will explore the emotional, spiritual, and financial tasks necessary to accomplish a "good" divorce.

What do we mean by a good divorce? Certainly we don't mean a painless one, since a painless divorce would be an oxymoron. But it is possible to separate from a spouse or long-term partner with a minimum of bitterness and hostility. It is possible to adhere to your own principles—not taking advantage of the other while at the same time ensuring that your rights are protected and your needs considered.

In the previous chapter we talked about the five principles that support a healthy relationship. These same five principles can support a healthy separation as well.

Generosity

During a separation, couples often feel anything but generous. It's all too easy to fall into the trap of either panic ("I'm taking care of number one. It's everyone for himself now.")

> Love is a feeling, marriage is a contract, and relationships are work.
> ~ **Lori Gordon, Marriage Therapist**

> Some of us think holding on
> makes us strong; but sometimes
> it is letting go.
> ~ Herman Hesse

or anger and vengeance ("I'll teach that #@&! by getting everything I possibly can.) Before taking action, though, pause and reflect. Five years from now, will you really be that concerned with who got the set of wine glasses? Does it make sense to win an extra $10,000 in the divorce settlement only to pay $9,500 of it to an attorney? Remember that you're fighting against the person you once loved—even if that's no longer the case. Most of all, remember that you'll have to live with yourself afterward. Do you want the self-image of a person who goes for the jugular?

On the other hand, maybe you're aware of co-dependent or self-sacrificing tendencies in yourself. Generosity also implies the art of being generous with yourself. It's fine—and even important—to let go of things that don't matter significantly in the long run. It's equally important, however, to protect those things that really matter to you. If you've been a stay-at-home wife and mother, for instance, it will be vitally important that you ensure an equitable settlement that will adequately support you and your children. If you've brought family heirlooms into the marriage, you will want to take any necessary steps to protect these things.

Primarily, generosity during a separation is a matter of attitude. If you take the approach that you want and expect a fair and reasonable settlement and if you are prepared to let go of the inconsequential in order to maintain a spirit of goodwill and cooperation, the chances of a "good" divorce are greatly increased.

Exercise: Assessing Your Priorities

This is an exercise that you can begin on your own, but it would be most helpful if shared with a friend.

Draw a vertical line down the center of a page in your Money Journal. Title one side of the page "Things I Can Let Go" and title the other side "Things That Really Matter to Me," then begin your lists. Write down everything that comes to mind, no matter how minor it might sound. These can be material possessions, family heirlooms and photographs, benefits like airline miles and timeshares ... anything you and your partner shared. When you feel your lists are complete, ask a trusted friend or therapist to look over them. Your friend may have some questions or thoughts about what you have written; listen with an open mind to the feedback. After hearing the feedback, you may want to revise your lists. These lists will provide you with a concrete reminder of what is really important to you when the separation negotiations start to feel overwhelming.

Empathy

Empathy may be the most difficult of the principles to maintain during this difficult period. It is vitally important to remember that everyone suffers during a separation. No matter who initiated the process, both sides feel pain and confusion, and you must work to maintain empathy for all concerned. If children are involved, their well-being must be a primary consideration during the separation process and afterward. You also need to pay attention to your own well-being. You need a lot of TLC right now, and self-denial is not an appropriate or helpful reaction. If you can take care of yourself while at the same time holding your partner in your heart, you are well on your way to moving through the separation with grace.

> Only your compassion and your loving kindness are invincible, and without limit.
> ~ Thich Nhat Hanh, Zen Teacher

In the midst of our client Sarah's divorce, she wore a T-shirt into her financial planning session that read: "There are two sides to every divorce: yours and the shithead's." We had a good laugh but eventually pointed out that this sentiment will not be helpful in the long run. There are definitely two sides to every divorce; the more you can appreciate your partner's without losing touch with your own, the more you'll be able to maintain an atmosphere of cooperation rather than antagonism.

Transparency

This principle takes on a somewhat different definition during a separation. At this point, it is no longer about transparency with your partner but rather transparency with yourself. What does this mean? Quite simply, it means being honest with yourself about your feelings, fears, grief, and needs. Even if the separation feels welcome to you, it is nevertheless a loss. If nothing more, it means the loss of a dream of fulfillment that you had when you joined with your partner. Allow yourself to acknowledge the grief. You may also have anger, anxiety, relief, confusion, and any number of different emotions. You may choose not to act on many of these emotions, but it's important to be patient with yourself as you ride the emotional rollercoaster. One day you may feel grief-stricken and fearful while the next you may feel free and light. Try to acknowledge the feelings without judging yourself.

Exercise: Emotional Journal

Begin a daily Emotional Journal. It is not important to write a lot in this journal at any one time, but it is good to be as consistent as possible. Without judging or editing, jot down comments about your emotional state each day. This exercise works well if done when you first wake up in the morning and/or just before you go to bed each night. Allow yourself to vent. Express all those thoughts and feelings you contain during the day. Your journal can be a safe place to express yourself without worrying about doing damage to anyone else. Over time, you will begin to see your feelings shift, and you will know that you are moving toward a place of healing.

Trust

Like transparency, the principle of trust should be applied to yourself more than to your partner during this time. It is important you learn to trust that:

1. Your thoughts and feelings *are* valid, even if they don't seem to make logical sense.
2. You *are* a person of innate value and worth, even when your self-esteem is taking a beating from the external world.

> Divorce is the psychological equivalent of a triple coronary by-pass. After such a monumental assault on the heart, it takes years to amend all the habits and attitudes that led up to it.
>
> ~ **Mary Kay Blakely,**
> **Journalist**

3. You *will* heal from the pain of the separation. You are making progress every day, though it is sometimes invisible to you.
4. You *can* have a satisfying, successful life without your ex-partner.
5. When the time is right, you *can* find another intimate relationship if you choose to.

You might want to use these five statements as affirmations. Make a copy of them and post it on your bathroom mirror so that you're confronted every day with positive thoughts. You are moving through "trial by fire," and since you are moving with consciousness you will emerge tempered and refined.

> Simply pushing harder within the old boundaries will not do.
> ~ **Karl Weick, Author**

Respect for Boundaries

Separation is, by definition, a shifting of boundaries. It's important to establish clear and respectful boundaries for yourself, your ex-partner, and your children, if any.

You may still feel very connected to your ex-partner. Perhaps the separation wasn't your choice, and you feel an urge to cling. Alternatively, perhaps you were the initiator of the separation and feel an urge to put as much distance as possible between him or her and yourself. While both of these feelings are understandable, avoid extremes in either direction.

Though you may have shared most of your feelings and experiences with your ex-partner during your time together, this is no longer appropriate. This is a time to deepen old friendships and develop new ones. You may want to find a therapist or support group to provide you with a sounding board, or you may find yourself turning more to your spiritual advisor and friends. Let yourself lean on others; you are retraining yourself to look elsewhere for help and comfort. This is especially important during the early days. Once the wounds of the separation have healed somewhat, you and your ex-partner may become good friends. This is not something that can be rushed, however. Allow distance at first. Both of you need time to recover and rebalance your lives.

In saying this, we don't mean to suggest that you cut off contact with your ex-partner completely. Communication around practical matters is vital. You will have many things to decide and divide, and it's far better to do this with a spirit of cooperation. To arrive at an agreement that feels fair, you may want to work with a mediator. This is a disinterested third party who will help you to talk about your needs without attacking each other. Some communities have collaborative law groups that provide couples with an attorney-therapist-mediator team to make the separation process non-adversarial.

Finally, if there are children involved, they also need to be protected by clear boundaries. This means that:

- The children are NEVER involved in discussions of adult concerns.
- The children's needs are the primary consideration in any sort of agreement made between you and your ex-partner.
- You and your ex-partner refrain from any negative comments about each other in the children's hearing.
- The children are NEVER asked to report on one parent to the other.
- Both you and your ex-partner cooperate in making reliable and flexible custody arrangements *for the children's benefit.*

The boundaries around the children will vary, of course, according to family circumstances and the children's ages. The important thing is that you and your ex-partner recognize the rights of the children to be loved, supported, and nurtured by both parents. Separation is inevitably difficult for them, and you will want to inform yourself as best you can about their developmental needs and the various

> Divorce. A resumption of diplomatic relations and rectification of boundaries.
> ~ **Ambrose Bierce, Writer**

ways of softening the blow for them. If given the proper support, however, your children—like you—can emerge from this period stronger and more resilient.

The Economics of Divorce

As we have seen throughout this book, emotional and financial matters cannot be separated; that which affects us emotionally affects us financially and vice versa. No life issue interweaves the emotional and financial aspects of life more than divorce. While the greatest cost of divorce is the emotional impact on the family, financial issues are a major concern. Here are eight practical steps that make sense in most divorces:

> If we don't stand up for children, then we don't stand for much.
> ~ **Marian Wright Edelman, Founder of the Children's Defense Fund**

1. Obtain a copy of your credit report. This is easy to do online through a number of services. The service we use is called *www.truecredit.com*. It is important in divorce to establish any debts that are outstanding. You do not want to finalize your divorce only to find that you owe on a debt that you did not even know existed.

2. Close your joint accounts; you do not want to become responsible for debts your spouse incurs while you are in the divorce process. And close these accounts in writing, making sure the financial institutions report to the credit bureaus that you have closed the accounts.

3. Open your own individual credit card accounts and bank accounts. It may be difficult to establish credit if you have been financially supported by your spouse and do not have your own credit history. It is better to open credit card accounts in your own name while you are still officially married.

4. Change the beneficiary on any retirement accounts, life insurance, or annuities. This is usually quite easy: Just call the financial institution in question, and they will send out a simple form.

5. Do not put your separate property into a jointly held account. Property that you brought into your marriage will generally be considered your separate property in divorce. Any property you put into a joint account, however, will likely be considered both of yours to be split up in a divorce settlement.

6. Be cautious in your negotiations concerning your spouse's retirement accounts; these can be very valuable. Do not trade them away without careful consideration from your financial advisor and divorce attorney.

7. If you keep the house, make sure you can continue to support it. Some women keep the house in order to protect their children from the pain of dislocation, only to find that they do not have the income to support the house. There is no way to totally protect your children from pain if you and your spouse divorce. Do not compound your problems by taking on the financial responsibility for a home that is too much for you. Ultimately, the children will do best in a home you can support financially.

8. Make sure that you continue to have health insurance (see our discussion of insurance in chapter 16). One medical event can have a devastating impact on your financial well-being. High deductible health insurance with a medical savings account may be a good way to go if you are in a financial squeeze. The last thing you need in the midst of a divorce is the financial devastation of a medical emergency. Make it a priority to pass that risk on to an insurance company by owning health insurance.

> One generation plants the trees; another gets the shade.
> ~ Chinese Proverb

The economics of divorce can be just as challenging as the emotional aspect. Taking the practical steps and adhering to the five principles through the emotional upheaval of a separation is far from easy. Be patient with yourself and don't expect to do it perfectly. Give yourself credit every day for the work you are doing in remaining conscious. Remind yourself of the Buddhist mantra "This too shall pass." The steps you are taking now to support yourself and your own development will pay large dividends in the years to come.

> When one door of happiness closes, another opens; but often we look so long at the closed door that we do not see the one which has been opened for us.
> ~ **Helen Keller, Writer**

HEALTHY FINANCIAL BOUNDARIES

8

Our discussion of healthy financial boundaries brings us to the heart of the interpersonal aspects of prosperity. We live amongst others always. In the economy of our intimate personal lives, there is a balance between sharing and limits. We support each other financially in healthy families, but we also set reasonable limits with each other. Insufficient financial support for the individual needs of a family member can cause one to miss important opportunities for achieving one's potential. Unlimited financial support, on the other hand, can undermine the family member's need to individuate, find their autonomy, and create a healthy separateness from the family. Healthy boundaries within a family help us to be close to each other by supporting our autonomy and individuality.

In order to achieve financial success you must set goals, stay committed to the goals over time, and be willing to set financial limits with yourself and others. Financial boundaries relate to the discipline it takes to achieve financial success. It takes healthy boundaries to say "yes" to a plan for your financial success. Likewise it takes healthy boundaries to say "no" to financial choices that will undermine your plans for success.

Being a smart investor also calls on you to have good boundaries; good investors avoid a herd mentality. When the herd is hot to buy a particular type of asset such as

> With boundaries, as in every area of the healing process, change starts with awareness.
> ~ **Robert Burney,**
> **Counselor**

technology stocks, it takes strong boundaries to hold to your investing principles, and avoid investing in "group-think."

In chapters 10 and 11 we go over sound investing principles and look at the kinds of mistakes investors tend to make when they succumb to the investing fad of the day rather than applying sound, proven investing principles. It takes healthy, strong boundaries to stay away from fad thinking; these strong boundaries will help you in many ways on your pathway to prosperity.

Defining Qualities of Financial Boundaries

What is a boundary in general? A boundary is a place where one thing ends and another begins. It is also a place where things are separated and connected. For example, if I stand at the fence-line between my property and my neighbor's, I am at the place that defines where our properties are separated. Looked at another way, the fence-line is the place where our properties meet. So a boundary has a dual quality: it is both a place that defines our separateness and at the same time defines where we meet.

Financial boundaries have the same dual quality as a fence-line: they define our financial separateness and our financial connectedness. We cannot have financial commitments without financial boundaries, as our financial boundaries define our financial commitments. Within our families we are connected to each other financially—we provide for our children. This is our financial connectedness. On the other hand, we don't provide unlimited resources for our children's every whim; this is our financial separateness. Healthy financial boundaries within the family provide needed support as well as reasonable limits.

We draw a boundary around ourselves and our families so that we can provide needed resources for each person's needs and development. For example, Mary is a professional woman and the mother of a six year old. Her husband died

> The boundary is where you experience the difference . . . where there is a "me" and a "you" . . . growth takes place when there is contact at the boundary.
>
> ~ Joseph C. Zinker, PhD,
>   Psychologist

in a car accident two years ago, leaving her with $200,000 in life insurance proceeds. The money is a resource for herself and her daughter, but she has drawn a boundary around the resource of the insurance money. That money will be used for her daughter's higher education, and Mary will not make it available for other purposes.

Why the focus on boundaries like these? They give shape to your life and commitments. With healthy boundaries surrounding your financial commitments, you can create a stable and resilient financial life.

Healthy and Unhealthy Financial Boundaries

Let's explore each of the characteristics of healthy and unhealthy financial boundaries with brief examples of each.

Healthy financial boundaries have a clear purpose.
Geoff and Judy have agreed to contribute $1,500 monthly to their retirement plan. The purpose of the retirement plan is to let them retire at sixty-five, providing enough money for them to live comfortably.

Unhealthy financial boundaries have a diffused purpose.
Jane and Larry sold their home in Los Angeles and moved to Scottsdale, Arizona, making a $150,000 profit in the move. They have defined no purpose for that money, and it is slowly dwindling away to pay for a new boat, elaborate vacations, and other luxury items they don't really need. Because their financial boundaries have diffuse purpose, they are squandering a valuable resource.

Healthy financial boundaries are characterized by strong commitment.
Jonathon and Martha have made a commitment to put $1,200 a month into their retirement savings. Last year, Martha had become interested in Pilates and wanted to buy

> I am responsible for what I do to others and for what I allow others to do to me.
> ~ Melody Beattie, Writer

a $1,500 Pilates table. Rather than forgo their commitment to their retirement or buy on credit, they waited a few months until they saved up enough to buy it with cash. Because their financial boundaries are characterized by strong commitment, they did not waver in funding their retirement plan.

Unhealthy financial boundaries demonstrate weak commitment.

> I am a man of fixed and unbending principles, the first of which is to be flexible at all times.
> ~ Everett Dirksen,
>   U.S. Senator

Sean and Elizabeth were saving up to buy their first home. It was a major goal for their family, and they had saved $20,000. Sean's brother racked up a number of serious gambling debts, and Sean used the entire $20,000 to bail out his brother. Now his family is back to square one in terms of saving for a home. Sean's financial boundaries were not clear and strong enough to withstand pressure from his family.

Healthy financial boundaries are flexible.
Geoff and Ellen are both teachers who are focused on saving for retirement. In recent years, Ellen has found that she is deeply drawn to developing a new career in law. Together, they have decided to draw from some of their retirement savings to fund her law school education. Although it took some soul-searching to make this decision, their flexibility allowed Ellen to pursue her dreams, and also was a good long-term investment in her future.

Unhealthy financial boundaries are overly rigid.
Jim is committed to keeping the family budget in line by keeping a tight grip on the family purse strings. When his teenage children ask him for money to pay for items they need, he becomes angry and makes them feel put-down for asking. His rigidity around money has engendered bad feelings in his family.

Healthy financial boundaries foster connections between people.

Stephen and Rita have been married for ten years. Stephen has a tendency to spend recklessly on "investments" (such as sports memorabilia) that always seem to lose money. Rita finally put her foot down, as his spending was getting out of control. Although Stephen became angry at first when she set limits with him, they soon started talking openly and honestly—for the first time—about the things they both needed in their marriage. They now talk often and openly about their lives, their marriage, and their financial lives. He found out that she needs financial security, and she found out that he needs his own space to pursue his hobbies. He still buys sports memorabilia but does so within a budget with which she is comfortable. Healthy financial boundaries made Stephen and Rita closer, and they both understand each other better.

> The best and most beautiful things in the world cannot be seen, nor touched . . . but are felt in the heart.
> ~ Helen Keller

Unhealthy financial boundaries cause alienation and bad feelings between people.

Bill made a small fortune in the oil and gas business. Unfortunately, he used his money to bully and run power trips on his wife and children. He used money to gain leverage rather than using it as a resource with which family members could work collaboratively. Bill's adult children now resent him, and there are numerous ugly feuds in the family.

Merger, Neglect, and Healthy Boundaries

We have seen the damage that overly rigid, alienating boundaries can cause. Equally dangerous are the extremes of merger and neglect.

Money Merger occurs when there is apparently no boundary between individuals in the family. It is a state of enmeshment in which it is unclear where one boundary ends and another begins. This state of merger frequently

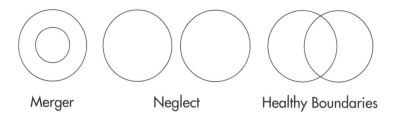

Merger   Neglect   Healthy Boundaries

> Your current safe boundaries were once unknown frontiers.
> ~ Anonymous

serves to protect from feelings of abandonment, seducing family members into never leaving home. It can be used to foster dependence and to shelter young adults in the family from the rough and tumble of establishing themselves in the world. Money Merger undermines the all-important process of financial individuation.

Money Neglect lies at the opposite polarity to Money Merger. It is a state of isolation in which the economic needs of individual family members are ignored. It is self-centeredness on the part of the family members with their hands on the family purse strings. It is a misuse of financial power in which individual needs are neglected. In such families, young people miss windows of opportunity for lack of financial support. The child with musical talent is not given desired music lessons, the young scholar is dissuaded from learning opportunities, the young athlete is told that playing on the team is just too costly. Lack of financial nurturance emanates from scarcity thinking; there is a fear that investment in personal development threatens the family's financial safety. With Money Neglect, safety and fear hold a tyrannical grip over the need for investment and nurturance.

Healthy financial boundaries are always in process within families. The goal is to find an optimal balance between providing financial support and fostering financial autonomy, and the choices are rarely perfect. These boundaries give family members the support they need—educationally, socially, medically, and so on—without undermining them in their journey to financial empowerment. Parents with healthy financial boundaries hold a firm expectation that children will contribute in some way to the family and become fully self-supporting in adulthood. Healthy boundaries set limits with family members while providing them with life-enhancing financial resources.

Unlike Money Merger and Money Neglect, healthy financial boundaries support your strength, autonomy, and individuality while supporting your intimate relationships and helping you to be close to others. Healthy boundaries will help you be a successful investor, and they will also help your family to be secure, strong, and independent. Your prosperity depends on strong, healthy, and flexible boundaries.

Happiness is not a matter of intensity but of balance and order and rhythm and harmony.

~ Thomas Merton, Trappist Monk, Writer

PART II
TRUE WEALTH

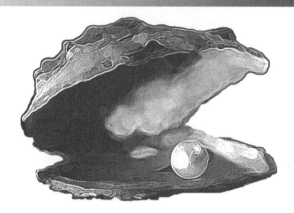

FUND YOUR FUTURE FIRST

9

Six Pillars of True Wealth
Smart Investing
Home Ownership
Empowered Earning
Conscious Spending and Credit
Adequate Insurance
Wise Planning

> If you have built castle(s) in the
> air, your work need not be lost;
> that is where they should be.
> Now put the foundations
> under them.
> ~ Henry David Thoreau

We've arrived at part II, where we cover the Six Pillars of True Wealth. This is where the rubber meets the road. Here we'll provide straightforward and uncomplicated guidelines that underlie financial success. As you apply them, you will find your financial life beginning to turn around. Any old sense of powerlessness in dealing with your financial affairs will give way to newfound confidence. Stress will yield to calm. Your Economic Self will go from flabby and out-of-shape to fit and trim.

If you find yourself stumped by any financial terminology in the chapters ahead, please refer to the glossary at the back of the book.

True Wealth awaits you! Let's get started on the first pillar of True Wealth, investing in your future.

Smart Investing

Financial work focuses your attention on your needs and on your emotional self-support. It emphasizes the need for healthy boundaries, clarity and empowerment. So, it should come as no surprise that the first pillar of True Wealth involves you putting your own financial needs first.

Many people think that the right thing to do is to pay their bills before they save for their future. We turn that thinking on its head: think about funding your future before you do anything else. Take it right off the top: fund your retirement plan first, and then take care of your other responsibilities. This one change will focus your financial life and help you take control. When you fund your future first, you pay yourself before you pay others. The earlier you do this, the more you will gain the leverage of time, which financial planners call the time value of money—one of the most powerful concepts in finance. We'll explore this concept in more detail in the next chapter. For now the important thing is that you put this powerful force to work for yourself by investing consistently over the long haul.

The best way to fund your future first is to set up an automatic investment plan with your payroll department or your bank. The money should go into a tax-deferred retirement account such as an IRA, a SEP IRA, or a 401(k) plan. Many companies offer a 401(k) plan. Nonprofits often have 403(b) plans, and some institutions offer 457 deferred compensation plans. One of the powerful things about automatic investing into a tax-deferred retirement account is that public policy supports your decision to do so with very favorable tax treatment. This gives your financial self-support a huge lift from the government.

Let's say that you and your spouse together gross $150,000 in 2007. With standard/itemized deductions and personal exemptions, that would put your taxable income at $133,100. Your marginal tax rate would be 28 percent. Your estimated federal income tax liability would be $26,672.

> No amount is too small when it comes to saving for the future. You're never too young, you're never too old. And you're never too broke.
>
> ~ Nancy Granovsky, Texas Cooperative Extension Family Economics Specialist

Without Tax-Deferred Investment		With Tax-Deferred Investment	
Joint Gross Income	$150,000.00	Joint Gross Income	$150,000.00
Total Amount Invested (adding together both spouses' 401[k] Plan contributions)	$ 0	Total Amount Invested (adding together both spouses' 401[k] Plan contributions)	$ 18,750.00
Taxable Income (after standard/itemized deductions & personal exemptions)	$133,100.00	Taxable Income (after standard/itemized deductions & personal exemptions)	$114,350.00
Marginal Tax Rate	28%	Marginal Tax Rate	25%
Estimated Federal Income Tax Liability	$ 26,672.00	Estimated Federal Income Tax Liability	$ 21,703.00

Tax Savings with a Tax-Deferred Investment Such as a 401(k)*

*Money withdrawn before age fifty-nine could result in a 10 percent early withdrawal penalty.

So, if you and your spouse gross $150,000 per year, you could pay $26,672 in income tax. That's a big chunk! But here is the good news: if you put 12.5 percent of your check into your 401(k) plans, then you have reduced your present taxation. You are now investing $18,750 per year in yourselves. The federal government will not tax that money until you retire and take the money out. With standard/itemized deductions and personal exemptions, that would reduce your taxable income to $114,350. Your marginal tax rate is reduced to 25 percent. Your estimated federal income tax liability is reduced to $21,703. You have in one fell swoop saved $18,750 for your future and deferred almost $5,000 in federal income taxes.

The illustration above shows how tax-deferred investing can help you save on taxes as you prepare for your future. We are big fans of tax-deferred investing and consider it one of the most powerful tools available to help you on your path to creating true wealth. We know, of course, that each situation is unique, so we have installed a handy tax calculator on our website, *www.insightfinancialgroup .com*. When you access the site, click on the Calculators link, choose Taxation, and then Income Tax. Simply plug in your information and the calculator will estimate how

The name of the game is taking care of yourself, because you're going to live long enough to wish you had.

~ Grace Mirabella

much tax savings you can expect by funding your tax-deferred account.

If your employer matches part of your 401(k) contributions, then we congratulate you for being in a position to accept free money! What could be better for wealth-building than money that is contributed by another party to your retirement account? We strongly recommend that you contribute at least enough to your retirement account to allow you to receive the full amount of any matching funds your employer offers.

Let's look at an example of what an employer match can do for your retirement savings over time. Our assumptions: an employee is thirty years old and will retire at sixty-five. She makes $40,000 per year and contributes 10 percent of her salary, or $4,000, per year. Her employer matches her contribution with $1,200 per year. If we assume a 7 percent rate of return over the years, her account will be worth $745,800 at retirement. Without the match, however, her account will be worth $573,691 at retirement. That is a difference of $172,109 for doing absolutely no extra work.

Let's look at tax-deferred investing another way, by comparing it to investing in a taxable account. To keep the arithmetic simple, let's suppose that you earn $100,000 per year and you are putting 15 percent of your gross income

> Contribute enough to make the most of any employer match. If you don't take advantage of the free money, it's like turning down a pay raise.
> ~ **Erin Burn, *Kiplinger's Personal Finance***

With Employer Match of $1,200		With No Employer Match	
Number of Years Making Contributions	35	Number of Years Making Contributions	35
Salary	$ 40,000.00	Salary	$ 40,000.00
Employee Contribution	$ 4,000.00	Employee Contribution	$ 4,000.00
Employer Match	$ 1,200.00	Employer Match	0
Assumed Rate of Return	7%	Assumed Rate of Return	7%
Future Value in 35 Years	$745,800.00	Future Value in 35 Years	$573,691.00

Positive Effects of an Employer Match on Your Retirement Plan*

*Employer contributions may be subject to a vesting schedule determined by the employer.

Prosperity is a way of living and thinking, and not just money or things. Poverty is a way of living and thinking, and not just a lack of money or things.

~ **Eric Butterworth, Minister**

We hope your eyes aren't glazing over, because all of this is critical as you build True Wealth. Please hang in there a little longer as we discuss what happens to your tax-deferred account when you retire and start to draw money out of it.

In retirement you will need to take out a required minimum distribution on your 401(k) each year and pay income taxes on the amount you take out. The money that stays in the account continues to grow tax-deferred. Let's stay with the value we have accumulated in the 401(k) described above: $1,015,147. Further, let's continue to assume a 7 percent return on money that is invested. Once you reach age seventy-and-a-half, the IRS requires that you take money out each year, so that they finally get some of the tax money you have been deferring all these years. In the table to the right you can see that at this rate, the projected account balance continues to grow, even while the required minimum distribution grows.

The point here is that you have reached critical mass in your tax-deferred account by the time you withdraw money for retirement. The amount you are earning with an assumed 7 percent growth keeps your account growing despite taking out the required minimum distribution each year. Your True Wealth is now literally paying dividends in a retirement that keeps on growing while providing you with income.

There is more good news. In a taxable account, capital gains and dividends are taxed. In your 401(k), capital gains and dividends are not taxed. Of course you will pay ordinary income taxes on the money when you take it out in retirement, but here lies another potential advantage: many people qualify for a lower income tax rate during retirement than they are assessed during their income earning years. It is therefore possible that when the money is ultimately taxed, you will be paying at a lower rate than your current rate. The fact that capital gains and dividends taxes are not assessed on your tax-deferred account works to your

into a 401(k). You would be investing $1,250 per month into your 401(k) for a total of $15,000 per year. Let's suppose that your average tax rate is 13.9 percent. If you invest in your 401(k), you can invest the entire $15,000. On the other hand, if you invest in a taxable account, you will have to pay income tax on that money, reducing your investment by the average tax rate of 13.9 percent. This calculates to $2,089 of taxes on your investment, reducing the amount invested to $12,911. Wouldn't you rather put that money to work for your future?

The differences really add up over time. Let's suppose that you earn an average of 7 percent on your investments. If you were to invest $15,000 each year for 25 years and achieve a 7 percent return, your future value in your 401(k) alone would be $1,015,147. What a nice path to True Wealth that is!

On the other hand, as we saw in the paragraph above, if you were to invest $15,000 per year for twenty-five years in your taxable account, only $12,911 would actually be invested each year due to the income taxes due. If you were to achieve the same 7 percent returns for twenty-five years, it would reduce your future value to $873,770. Additionally, your capital gains and dividends would be subject to taxation throughout that twenty-five-year period.

> The avoidance of taxes is t
> only intellectual pursuit th
> carries any rewar
> ~ John Maynard Keynes
> Economis

Taxable Investment Account		Tax-Deferred Investment Account		
Gross Invested Amount	$ 15,000.00	Gross Invested Amount	$	15,000.0
Federal Income Tax Due (@ 13.9 % average tax rate)	$ 2,089.00	Federal Income Tax Due (@ 13.9 % average tax rate)	$	-
Total Amount Invested Annually	$ 12,911.00	Total Amount Invested Annually	$	15,000.
25 years of investing $12,911 each year @ 7% return	$873,770.00	25 years of investing $12,911 each year @ 7% return	$1,015,147.	
Amount subject to capital gains and dividend taxes?	Yes	Amount subject to capital gains and dividend taxes?		

Future Value of Taxable Investing vs. Tax-Deferred Investing*

*This chart is for illustrative purposes only. Rates of return are hypothetical, do not reflect the performance of an actual investment, and should not be considered a guarantee of future performance.

Year	Projected Account Balance	Required Minimum Distribution
2006	$1,015,147.00	$37,049.16
2007	$1,049,158.13	$39,590.87
2008	$1,083,008.33	$42,305.01
2009	$1,116,513.90	$45,202.99
2010	$1,149,466.88	$48,296.93
2011	$1,181,632.63	$51,599.68
2012	$1,212,747.23	$55,124.87
2013	$1,242,514.67	$58,609.18
2014	$1,270,881.52	$62,605.00
2015	$1,297,238.23	$66,525.04
2016	$1,321,519.87	$70,669.51
2017	$1,343,356.75	$75,047.86
2018	$1,362,343.86	$79,669.23
2019	$1,378,038.70	$84,542.25
2020	$1,389,959.16	$89,674.78
2021	$1,397,581.52	$94,431.18
2022	$1,400,981.05	$99,360.36

> If you have built castles in the air, your work need not be lost; that is where they should be. Now put the foundations under them.
> ~ **Henry David Thoreau**

Required Minimum Distribution Schedule*

*This assumes a 7 percent return.[1]

advantage. It takes a drag off of your earnings and lets compounding occur more efficiently. In other words, making future profits from your present profits can happen more efficiently if you don't have to take money out of your account each year to pay taxes on those profits.

---

1 Figures derived from the Putnam Investments website Required Minimum Distribution Calculator. Assumptions: 7 percent return on invested funds. Distribution schedule is for Single Life Certain. Monies withdrawn before age 59½ could result in a 10 percent early withdrawal penalty.

The journey of a thousand miles must begin with a single step.
~ Lao-Tzu

Self-employed Retirement Plans

For self-employed people, there are two retirement plans we especially like. The first is a SEP IRA. The self-employed person is allowed to contribute up to 20 percent of his or her net self-employed profits, up to $44,000. Net profits for the SEP IRA are calculated in the following way: subtract one-half of your self-employment taxes from your net self-employment income. Then multiply the resulting self-employment income by 20 percent to get your contribution limit. You can easily figure your SEP contribution amount with your tax advisor's input, or if you use tax-preparation software such as TurboTax, it will instantly calculate your contribution limits. We have also posted the relevant IRS publication on our website, *www.insightfinancialgroup.com*. Click on the Tax Center and then Tax Forms. Form 590 explains the SEP IRA in straightforward language. We also offer information on all the other tax-deferred plans.

Another great option for self-employed people is the Individual 401(k). We like this plan for a number of reasons. First, it has more generous contribution limits than the SEP IRA. With the Individual 401(k), the self-employed person is not limited to contributing 20 percent of his or her net income, a number that some self-employed people try to keep low in order to minimize taxes. Instead, the self-employed person is considered both the employer and the employee. As an employee, you can contribute up to $15,000 in 2006. If you are fifty years old or older, you can contribute another $5,000 per year. As an employer, you can contribute up to 25 percent of your earned income. The combined maximum contribution for the Individual 401(k) is $44,000 per year, or $49,000 if you are fifty-years-old or older. Again, it is important to go over the best kind of plan with your financial planner or tax adviser. Public policy strongly supports tax-deferred investing for the self-employed person, and we think that is a royal road to prosperity.

Individual Retirement Accounts (IRAs)

An IRA is a retirement account that you invest in on your own, outside of your employment. Certain rules apply as to whether you can deduct the contribution or not: they take into account your age, whether you participate in a retirement plan at work, and your income. Rather than go over these rules, we have posted a handy calculator on our website. Simply go to *www.insightfinancialgroup.com*, click on the Calculators link, Retirement, and then click the IRA Eligibility calculator. It will tell you whether you qualify and how much you can contribute. In 2006 the maximum annual contribution to an IRA was $4,000 for people younger than fifty and $5,000 for people fifty and older. An IRA is a great place for you to get started with your retirement planning—especially if you don't have a tax-deferred retirement plan at work.

> Destiny is not a matter of chance but of choice. Not something to wish for but to attain.
> ~ **William Jennings Bryan, American Lawyer, Statesman**

Traditional vs. Roth

There are two basic varieties of tax-advantaged contributions to your retirement fund: Traditional and Roth. Both are given favorable treatment by the IRS, but they work differently. This chapter has so far focused on traditional contributions. In a Traditional contribution you invest with pre-tax money and then pay ordinary income tax on the money you withdraw in retirement. Roth contributions are just the opposite. You pay into the retirement account with after-tax money, but then you never have to pay taxes on this money—the principal or the growth—again. Roth contributions have been available for many years with IRAs, they are available in 401(k) accounts as well.

Although we are huge proponents of traditional tax-deferred contributions, under certain circumstances, the Roth can be a great way to go. First, the Roth will provide you with a source of tax-free funds in retirement.[2] No taxes

---

2 Ordinary income taxes are paid on gains, dividends, or interest if held in the account for less than five years or withdrawn prior to age fifty-nine-and-a-half. Also, withdrawals are subject to a 10 percent early withdrawal penalty and ordinary income tax if distributed before age fifty-nine-and-a-half.

are paid on gains, dividends, or interest—ever. That is a huge benefit. Second, since you do not pay taxes on the Roth money when you take it out in retirement, it does not count as ordinary income in retirement. This means that you are less likely to have to pay taxes on your social security benefits because your taxable income will not have been raised. Third, the Roth IRA does not require you to take money out in retirement (required minimum distributions) the way traditional plans do, as we described above. It is more flexible than the Traditional IRA in this respect.

The Roth IRA is also good for your beneficiaries. At your death, your beneficiaries receive the proceeds of your Roth tax-free. In contrast, your heirs would have to pay income taxes on the money inherited from 401(k)s and Traditional IRAs. Another Roth advantage: you can take your principal out without penalty. With a Traditional IRA, you must pay a penalty to the IRS for early withdrawal. Say, for example, you invested $4,000 this year in your Roth IRA, and you've gained $500 from your investments. You can take out the $4,000 without penalty before you reach the age of fifty-nine-and-a-half. In a Traditional IRA you would need to wait until that age to do the same without penalty.

Here's yet another possible advantage of the Roth: some people think that income tax rates will rise in the future due to high deficits and the retirement of millions of baby boomers, putting new financial pressures on our society. If income tax rates go up, Roth owners will have the advantage of having paid the lower rate when they made the original contribution, and will avoid the higher rates of the future. Of course, this is speculative—it is also possible that income tax rates will stay steady or even go down.

Should you go with a Traditional or Roth IRA? First, check our calculator to ascertain your eligibility for either or both (*www.insightfinancialgroup.com*). From our perspective, we want you to get started with either one. They are

New rules will soon allow many more retirement savers to have a Roth IRA. My advice is "go for it."
~ Walter Updegrave,
Senior Editor of
Money Magazine

both greatly advantageous over taxable investing, and both are immeasurably better than no investing at all. There are many choices in the area of tax-advantaged investing. Most people will benefit from meeting with a qualified, ethical financial planner to make informed decisions about the best way to go. He or she can help you set up the kind of tax-deferred plan that will work best in your unique situation.

Tax-advantaged investing is an invaluable resource in building True Wealth. The question now arises: Where am I going to find the money to fund my tax-deferred account? The answer to this is a holistic one—it involves your money script, your earning, and your spending. We will be covering earning and spending later in the book, but let us simply preview that discussion with the following statement: *It's not just how much you earn; it's how much of what you earn that you keep!*

> One of the smartest money moves a young person can make is to invest in a Roth IRA.
> ~ *Kiplinger's Personal Finance* magazine

That statement is so obvious and simple that it's laughable, right? Yes, but that does not make it any less powerful. You can make big money and still be broke if your spending is out of control. On the other hand, you can make a middle-class income and do quite well financially if you keep your spending under control and invest consistently and wisely over time. In the financial world, it is not uncommon for the tortoise to come out better in the long run than the hare. Fortunately all the psychological work we have done in part I of this book has prepared you to look at yourself and your habits with an accepting yet disciplined eye.

You've just learned the first rule of building True Wealth: fund your future first. We strongly suggest that you have a discussion with your employer about their tax-deferred investing plan. Most employers have a 401(k) or similar plan that you can invest in. If you are self-employed, then you have an even greater opportunity to put pre-tax money away by setting up your own retirement plan. The key is to get started now and hang in there for the long haul.

Exercise: Anxieties and Anticipations

Start a new page in your Money Journal. Draw a line down the center of the page and label one side of the page "Anxieties." Label the other side "Anticipations." On the Anxieties side begin a list of the negative thoughts and feelings that arise when you think about automatic investing. For example: "I'll feel deprived—no more 'extras' in the budget." Or: "I'm afraid I won't be able to pay my bills—the credit card companies will be breathing down my throat!" Or maybe: "I'll feel like things are out of my control—money 'disappearing' every month, even into my own account for my own benefit, feels scary to me."

When your list feels complete for the moment, consider each item on the Anxieties list. Take a moment just to breathe. Remember not to succumb to a Superego Attack for having these anxieties. It's only natural to feel uncertainty and a lack of confidence when embarking on a new venture. Remind yourself that you can move as slowly as you need to. Give yourself lots of positive reinforcement for each step forward (including making this list!).

Now turn your attention to the Anticipations side of the page. This is the place to let yourself dream. What would it be like to have a comfortable portfolio? One example response is: "If I put enough away, I could retire at fifty-five and travel." Or: "This is the money that could fund the lake cabin my wife and I would love to build after retirement." Read through each of the Anticipation items. Allow yourself to feel the excitement that arises as you look toward realizing your dreams. With automatic investing you are taking a significant step toward the creation of true wealth.

In Summary

In this chapter you've learned the importance of funding your retirement plan before you pay out money to others. You've seen the great advantages to automatically investing each month in a tax-advantaged retirement account. In brief, here are the things you need to remember:

- Invest automatically in a tax-advantaged account each and every month.

> Tomorrow belongs to the people who prepare for it today.
> ~ **African Proverb**

- Over time, the benefits of a tax-advantaged account over a taxable account really add up.
- Take advantage of employer contributions if your company offers them.

We are called to be architects of the future, not its victims.

~ R. Buckminster Fuller, Inventor, Visionary

SMART INVESTING:
Stock Market

<u>Six Pillars of True Wealth</u>
Smart Investing
Home Ownership
Empowered Earning
Conscious Spending and Credit
Adequate Insurance
Wise Planning

> There are two kinds of investors, those who know they can't predict the market and those who don't know that they can't predict the market.
> ~ **William Bernstein, Investment Writer**

You can predict that the stock market will go up and down, but you can't predict when. In a "bull market," stock prices are generally rising. In a "bear market," stock prices are generally falling. Prices will inevitably rise and fall—such is the nature of the stock market. Smart investors know this and take advantage of the fact. It's actually quite easy to do so using the tools we give you in this book.

The stock market is in constant motion, responding to an ever-changing set of conditions. Economic and political factors such as interest rates, taxation policies, and the business cycle all influence the stock market, with international political factors and intangibles such as the psychology of investors. There are too many factors at play for any one human being to predict when the market will go up or go down. Many people present themselves as capable of predicting when the stock market will rise or fall, but the truth is that no one can predict—not us, not you, and not the most highly paid guru on Wall Street. The good news is that this puts you on an equal footing with other investors. The bad news is that inexperienced investors frequently imagine that they can predict or "time" the market. Unfortunately this strategy frequently leads them to *buy high* and *sell low*. In this chapter we will introduce you to easily implemented strategies to avoid this trap and to take advantage of the stock market's short-term unpredictability.

> Our favorite holding period is forever.
> ~ **Warren Buffett, Investor, Businessman**

Buy Automatically Each Month

We strongly advise against trying to "time the market"; that is, waiting to invest until you feel that the market, or a particular stock, is going to rise in value. Instead, we recommend that you invest automatically each and every month, whether the market is up or down. With automatic investing, you invest a given dollar amount each month into your portfolio of securities (stocks, bonds, mutual funds, and so on), regardless of current stock market conditions.

Let us suppose you have implemented a plan to invest $1,000 dollars per month into your retirement portfolio within your 401(k). This way you will automatically buy more shares when the price is low, fewer when the share price is high. Because you accumulate more shares for your money when the market is down, your average cost per share will be less than the average market price per share in fluctuating markets. Automatic investing involves continuous investment in securities, regardless of fluctuation in price levels.

Regular investing does not ensure a profit and does not protect against loss in declining markets. You should consider your ability to invest continuously during periods of fluctuating price levels.

Keep Buying When Stocks Are on Sale

If you continue to invest through changing market conditions, automatic investing can be an effective way to accumulate assets to meet your long-term goals. It makes sense to make the *accumulation* of shares your goal. You will then be looking forward to the next downturn in the stock market. Inexperienced investors react with fear to downturns in the market, but smart investors know that those periods provide an opportunity to buy shares that are on sale. Stock market downturns are good for the investor who is buying because in a down market—when stock prices are cheaper—you get more shares for your money. Just as if you budget $100 per month for clothing, you can purchase more and better clothing with your money if you buy when the clothing store is having a sale. Furthermore, those same mutual fund shares that you bought when the market was down could be more valuable when the market has its next upswing.

Nobody knows what will happen in the stock market tomorrow. However, we have a long history of evidence showing that the stock market has been, over the long haul, the strongest place to make your money grow. The average annual return on investments in stocks measured by the S&P 500 from 1928 to 2005 has been a healthy 13.02 percent.[1] If history is any measure, stocks will continue to be an important part of your path toward true wealth. The stock market is a place where there is fluctuation in the short run and a history of long-term growth. The key then is to be tolerant of the short-term fluctuations so you can participate in long-term growth.

> Don't get into market timing. Your emotions always lead you the wrong way. I would say the best rule for most investors is, stay the course.
> ~ **John C. Bogle, Founder of the Vanguard Group**

Exercise: Investing and Emotions

Part of the focus of this chapter is to support you in separating your investing strategy from your emotions. Take out your Money Journal and think about the following question. Try not to think too hard about your answers—just allow yourself to write in a stream-of-consciousness style.

Given what you know about yourself and your money script, what are your vulnerabilities when it comes to making investment decisions?

---

1 Aswath Damodaran, PhD. pages.stern.nyu.edu/~adamodar/pcdatasets /histretSP.xls

For instance:

- The Hoarder might find it difficult to part with money, even when it's for investment purposes. (Daisy's mother kept a stash of cash—at one point almost $100,000—hidden in the house. Intellectually she knew it didn't make sense, but she needed the feeling of security it gave her.)
- The Co-Dependent might find himself searching for "an expert" and following the advice of others at the expense of listening to his own wisdom and common sense.
- The Power Player might trust *too much* in her own instincts, believing that she knows better than anyone and refusing to ask for help or advice.
- The Coupon Clipper might be unwilling to pay for any financial help or advice, believing that it's foolish to "waste" money on something he can do himself.
- The Gambler may be attracted to the risks of using her investment portfolio as the stake in a dangerous game of chance.
- The Masquerader may be reluctant to use some of his "keeping up appearances" money for investing in the future.

> Emotions take over for most of us, and frequently cloud our judgment, making it hard to see the mistakes we make.
> ~ Hannah Ricci,
> Financial Writer

By this point, you have done a lot of work toward increasing your understanding of yourself. You have a greater awareness of your strengths and your vulnerabilities. Hopefully, you are becoming more comfortable with exploring your "shadow"—the part we all carry that we like to keep hidden from the world. Be careful as you explore that you don't succumb to Superego Attacks and start critiquing yourself. Rather, deal with your vulnerable self the way a kind parent would deal with a child—supportive and encouraging, yet expecting continued growth.

Be a Long-Term Investor in Mutual Funds

It is not only much simpler to be a long-term investor than an active trader, it is a far more effective strategy for most investors. Mutual funds can be an excellent vehicle for your long-term investments. If you work with a financial planner, he or she can help you pick out a portfolio of mutual funds that will be appropriate for you. There are of course numerous sources of information online as well, including Yahoo Finance (*www.finance.yahoo.com*), MSN money (*www.money.msn.com*), The Motley Fool (*www.fool.com*), and Morningstar (*www.morningstar.com*). Mutual funds are an excellent tool for you on your pathway toward True Wealth because they can provide diversification, asset allocation, ease of use, and automatic investing. Of course, not all mutual funds are created equal, so at the end of this chapter we will provide you some guidance and more resources for choosing the best mutual funds for you and your unique situation.

> The four most dangerous words in investing are "This time it's different."
> ~ Sir John Templeton, Businessman, Philanthropist

Diversifying Among Asset Classes

In the language of financial planning, an "asset" is anything you own that has cash value. Examples are stocks, bonds, mutual funds, real estate, and cash. An "asset class" is a category of investments such as U.S. Growth Stocks, U.S. Government Bonds, Foreign Stocks, or a Money Market Fund. Obviously there are many different asset classes, but there are certain asset classes that are commonly held in retirement accounts. These include the categories in the table on the next page.

Don't Put All Your Eggs in One Basket

There is a lot about investing that nobody can predict. For example, although any investment adviser can tell you which of the above asset classes did best last year, no one can predict with any degree of certainty which will do better *next year*. Therefore, it is best to stay invested in all the major asset classes over the long haul. That way, you won't be chasing last year's winner, which may be tomorrow's loser. Many people made the mistake during the late-1990s "tech bubble" of putting all their eggs in the tech stock basket, only to end up with a lot of broken eggs when those stocks dropped

Stocks	Bonds	Cash	Specialty
Value stocks	Government bonds	Money market	Real estate
Growth stocks	Investment-grade corporate bonds	CDs	Oil and gas
Foreign stocks	Government agency bonds	Bank accounts	
Large-cap stocks	High-yield (Junk) bonds		
Mid-cap stocks	Municipal bonds		
Small-cap stocks			

> It pays to be as broadly diversified as possible.
> ~ Jeremy Siegel, Economist

sharply in the early-2000s. Any asset class, including real estate, will have its good years and its bad years. Fortunately, you don't have to be an expert in any of these asset classes—there are sound, well-managed mutual funds in every major asset class. The mutual fund manager picks the individual securities, such as stocks and bonds, that are held in the fund; you or your adviser picks the fund that covers that particular asset class.

Diversification Adds Stability to Your Portfolio

The Nobel Prize–winning economist Harry Markowitz made some remarkable observations about investing. He looked beyond the picking of individual stocks, which previously had dominated investment thinking, and considered creating overall portfolios that are efficient in terms of generating maximum return for a given degree of risk. His approach, known as Modern Portfolio Theory, is highly influential among investment professionals and is a widely respected approach to investing.

Markowitz noted that certain stocks have an inverse correlation to each other in terms of price. For a simplified, hypothetical example, let's say that high gold prices are good for a gold mining company but bad for a gold jewelry manufacturer. The high gold prices are good for the mining company because it earns more for its raw gold. The high price of gold is bad for the jewelry company because it needs to pay more for the raw material that its product is made of, cutting into its profits. As an investor, you will attain better diversification if you invest in a gold mining company and a gold jewelry company than if you invest in two gold mining companies or two gold jewelry companies. This is because the gold mining company and gold jewelry company have a low correlation to each other. When one goes down, the other tends to go up and vice versa. An investment portfolio with good diversification will weather changes in market conditions better than a portfolio where there is limited diversification. The issue of diversification brings us back to the importance of your asset allocation. A portfolio with a proper asset allocation for your needs is a diverse portfolio that will help you achieve your financial goals.

> The biggest risk of all is failing to diversify properly.
> ~ **William Bernstein,**
> **Physician,**
> **Investment Writer**

Asset Allocation

Asset allocation is an investment strategy to diversify your investments among a variety of asset classes. The essential idea behind asset allocation is to align your investment portfolio with your life goals while:

1. staying invested in the market;
2. diversifying your investments.

A qualified financial adviser will be well-versed in asset allocation strategies. He or she can help you design and implement an asset allocation that aligns with your tolerance for risk and your life circumstances. Some asset allocations are more aggressive, while others are more conservative. The latter will be more volatile with greater potential for growth while the former will be less volatile but have less growth potential. Should your portfolio be more aggressive or more conservative? In general, the

Individuals ought to concentrate on using the market more than beating it. Focus on questions of asset allocation, diversification, and changes through time.

~ **William Sharpe, Economist**

closer you are to needing the money, the more conservative you should be in your asset allocation. If you are saving for retirement, your portfolio should become more conservative as you approach retirement. Another general statement: The more conservative your investment, the greater the percentage of bonds and cash you should have in your portfolio. The more aggressive you are, the more you will want stocks in your portfolio. We have put a useful asset allocation calculator on our website (*www.insightfinancialgroup.com*) to give you some orientation as to an asset allocation that would fit for your risk tolerance and your life circumstances.

	Aggressive	Moderately Aggressive	Moderate	Moderately Conservative	Conservative
Money Market	5%	5%	10%	15%	20%
Real Estate	5%	5%	5%	10%	10%
Government Bonds			5%	10%	20%
Investment-Grade Bonds		10%	15%	20%	20%
High Yield Bonds	5%	10%	10%	15%	20%
Large-Cap Value	10%	10%	10%	10%	5%
Mid-Cap Value	10%	10%	10%	5%	
Small-Cap Value	15%	10%	5%		
Large-Cap Growth	10%	10%	10%	10%	5%
Mid-Cap Growth	10%	10%	10%	5%	
Small-Cap Growth	15%	10%	5%		
International	15%	10%	5%		

To the left are examples of asset allocations for five different risk tolerances: aggressive, moderately aggressive, moderate, moderately conservative, and conservative. We are including them just to give you an illustration, not to recommend these asset allocations specifically.

If you look at the five asset allocations you will see that as we grow increasingly aggressive, we invest more heavily in stocks, whereas the more conservative we become, the more we invest in bonds. In the most aggressive portfolio, stocks comprise 85 percent of the asset allocation. In the most conservative portfolio, stocks make up just 10 percent.

Exercise: Take a Break

How are you feeling at this point? If you've been reading steadily, you may be feeling a little overwhelmed mentally and emotionally and a little cramped in your body. This is a good time to take a break. Go outdoors for a short walk if you can. Make yourself a cup of tea. Take a few moments just to check in with yourself—pay attention to your breath, do a few stretches, center yourself, and remind yourself of why you are doing this work. The whole purpose behind this book is providing you with the emotional support, psychological understanding, and practical knowledge you need to access your own inner wisdom. We all have this wisdom. Remind yourself that you are taking important steps toward becoming more in touch with it.

Stocks, Bonds, Mutual Funds, and Risk

Stocks

When you buy a stock, you are buying partial ownership in a corporation. For example, if you buy 100 shares of GE, you are buying a (very, very small) fraction of ownership in GE. You buy stocks through a stock exchange such as the New York Stock Exchange or the NASDQ. When you buy stock in a corporation there are two potential sources of profits: dividends and capital appreciation. Dividends are proportional shares of corporate profits that are paid out to shareholders. Not all common stocks pay dividends—

> It is a kind of spiritual snobbery that makes people think that they can be happy without money.
> ~ Albert Camus, Author, Philosopher

many do not. Corporations are under no obligation to pay dividends to shareholders of common stocks. Certain kinds of corporations such as utilities, banks, and insurance companies tend to pay dividends. The second source of profits is capital appreciation. If the price of the stock goes up and you sell it when it is up from the price at which you bought it, then you have achieved capital appreciation with that stock. Of course, stock prices can and do go up and down, so capital appreciation is by no means guaranteed.

> Investors have traditionally held bonds in their portfolio for three reasons: income, diversification, and protection against economic weakness.
> ~ Bill Gross, Investment Manager

Bonds

A bond is a loan. When you buy a bond, you are basically making a loan to the issuer. Corporations, the federal government, and municipalities all issue bonds in order to raise money. Let's say for example that the city of New York wants to raise money to build a new bridge. They might issue a series of bonds for that purpose. The city sets the terms of the bonds, and if those terms are attractive to investors, thousands of the bonds will be sold. The city will pay investors the interest rate that has been stipulated at the outset. After a given period of time, the bonds will mature and the city will pay back the principal. Because bonds are essentially loans, they generally are more conservative investments than stocks.

With bonds, as with all investments, investors want greater return for taking greater risk. If Wal-Mart issues a bond, that bond is a relatively low-risk investment because Wal-Mart is perceived to be a strong company. Wal-Mart therefore can pay a relatively lower interest rate. If a company that is perceived to be on shaky ground—Kmart, for example—issues a bond, it will have to pay a higher interest rate. If investors can get the same interest rate from a Wal-Mart bond that they can get from a Kmart bond, they will buy the Wal-Mart one because Wal-Mart is perceived to be better able to pay that loan back. Kmart has to pay a higher interest rate because buying a loan from them is riskier, and investors want to be rewarded for taking risk.

Bonds are rated for their riskiness by companies like Standard & Poors and Moodys. The riskier the bond, the higher the interest rate the issuer has to pay in order to interest investors in buying it. Your asset allocation will likely include bonds of a few different varieties such as government bonds, high-yield bonds (also known as "junk bonds") and lower risk bonds (also known as "investment-grade bonds"). If you look at the five asset allocations on page 124, you will see these various bond asset classes comprising differing percentages of the asset allocation depending on the overall risk profile of the portfolio. Bonds play an important role in the creation of True Wealth. As you get closer to retirement, bonds should comprise a greater percentage of your portfolio—they can add stability to your asset allocation.

> It pays to be as broadly diversified as possible.
> ~ Jeremy Siegel, Professor of Finance, Wharton School

Mutual funds

If all this talk about stocks and bonds has you feeling a little overwhelmed, take heart. You don't need to be an expert in stocks and bonds to be an effective investor. Mutual funds offer professional management of stocks and bonds in portfolios that bring the buying power of many investors together. Mutual funds are widely used by wealthy investors as well as middle-class people who are saving for retirement. Each mutual fund deals with a distinct asset class or balance of asset classes. As an individual investor, you do not need to buy and sell stocks and bonds. You can let the mutual fund manager do that. Instead, you decide on an appropriate asset allocation and you find well-managed mutual funds that cover each of the asset classes you need.

For each asset class we have described in the five asset allocations on page 124, there are many mutual funds that specialize in that asset class. So, for example, if you need to put 20 percent of your portfolio into government bonds, you can find a mutual fund specializing in that asset class with a variety of mutual funds companies. Look for mutual funds that have low expense ratios and good ratings by Morningstar (*www.morningstar.com*). MSN Money (*www.money.msn.com*) also has excellent information on mutual funds, including each mutual fund's Morningstar rating.

Mutual funds are an essential tool in your journey toward True Wealth. They give you access to professional money managers who can bring the full resources of their respective firms to your investments. Mutual funds also make it much easier to implement your asset allocation strategy. Since each mutual fund covers a particular asset class, the process of implementing your allocation of asset classes is greatly simplified. Rather than having to analyze hundreds of stocks and bonds to fit into your strategy, you simply find well-managed mutual funds for each asset class and let the manager of each mutual fund analyze the individual stocks and bonds.

> There's no escaping risk. Once you decide to put your money to work to build long-term wealth, you have to decide, not whether to take risk, but what kind of risk you wish to take.
>
> ~ John C. Bogle, Founder of the Vanguard Group

Risk

Risk is a fundamental reality of investing. When you make an investment, you are taking a risk. You hope the investment will appreciate and that your investment will pay off, but you are aware that there is always the risk that the investment will lose value or even become totally worthless. The price of any stock can go to zero if the company goes out of business. Of course, it is far less likely that GE will go out of business than a new internet-based company. Therefore, buying the stock of a established, large Blue Chip company like GE is usually considered less risky than buying the stock of a new, relatively small company. On the other hand, that company may have the potential for more growth in its stock price than a mature company like GE. There is no getting away from risk in the world of investing.

There is a relationship in the investing world between risk and reward. If you buy a CD at the bank, you can feel pretty certain that your investment won't lose value. It is a low-risk investment, and therefore the potential reward is less than that of buying the stock of a company which has the potential to pay dividends and increase in value. When you buy stock in a small internet company that might become the next Amazon.com, you are making a high-risk investment, and you are trading high risk for potentially high reward. The best of all worlds is an investment with low risk and high reward. The worst of all worlds is an investment with high risk and low rewards.

Socially Responsible Investing

Many of our financial planning clients are concerned that their investments reflect their social, political, and spiritual values. They are aware that money represents energy that can be put to positive or negative uses. If you share these concerns, then socially responsible investing may be of interest to you. Whether you are invested in mutual funds, variable life insurance, annuities, or individually managed accounts, socially responsible investment alternatives are available. The burgeoning field of socially responsible investing (known in the industry by the acronym SRI) has attracted thousands of investors and billions in capital. An excellent clearinghouse of information on SRI funds and advisers is *www.socialfunds.com*.

> We have a responsibility to look after our planet. It is our only home.
> ~ **His Holiness the Dalai Lama**

Socially responsible investing generally works by way of screening. An SRI mutual fund will invest in companies that meet its investment criteria just as any mutual fund does. Additionally, the SRI fund will screen for corporate behavior. Each SRI fund has its own measures for the corporate behavior they will screen out. An SRI fund may screen out investing in companies that engage in weapons manufacturing, poor environmental practices, use of child labor, discriminatory practices, and so on. Another method that some SRI funds use is shareholder advocacy. The SRI fund will purchase shares of a company and sponsor shareholder resolutions to influence corporate behavior. SRI funds thus allow investors to align their investment dollars with their principles. If you are a person with deeply felt social concerns, SRI investing may encourage you to get more involved with your economic life.

The Time Value of Money

The time value of money states that the longer you have to invest your money, the more your money can work for you. If you won a $50,000 prize from the Publishers Clearing House, would you rather have the payment now, or a year from now? Most people would rather have it now. The reasons for this are many. First, if you wait a year, there is the possibility that the Publishers Clearing House will go out of business. Second, there is inflation. On the day that we are writing this, the current inflation rate is 3.5 percent, so your prize a year from now would be worth $48,250 in today's dollars. Third, there is the interest you could receive if you invested the money. On the day that we are writing this, one-year CDs are being offered at 5.2 percent APY, which means that in one year, if you bought a CD with her winnings, your $50,000 investment would be valued at $52,662.28. Finally, and most importantly, there is the power of compounding. If the CD you bought with your prize is worth $52,662.28 after one year, then you have that amount available the next year to buy a new CD. For all of these reasons, the time value of money is a very powerful principle in the creation of true wealth. The sooner you begin your investment program, the more you can put the time value of money to work for you.

Compounding Your Earnings

Compounding is one thing that makes the time value of money such a powerful tool. With compounding, you make money on your profits. The difference between simple interest and compound interest is this: with simple interest, your interest is calculated on the amount you initially invested,

> Do not squander time for that is the stuff life is made of.
> ~ Benjamin Franklin

whereas with compound interest your interest is calculated on the amount you invested plus the amount your investment has earned. Compound interest is more advantageous in terms of building wealth—and far more advantageous in building wealth over time.

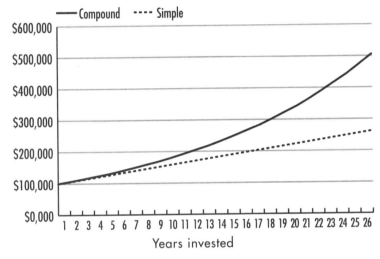

Simple vs Compound Interest

6.5 interest rate invested over 25 years—compounded monthly

The most powerful force in the universe is compound interest.
~ **Albert Einstein**

The chart above shows the difference between compound versus simple interest if you were to invest $100,000 over twenty-five years at a 6.5 percent interest rate. After twenty-five years with simple interest, the value would be $262,500.00. On the other hand, after twenty-five years with compound interest, the value would be $505,619.78. We've charted the difference above so you can see visually what happens over time. Notice that the two lines start the same, but over time the compound rate gets farther and farther ahead of the simple rate as the compounding works its magic.

By beginning your investing program early, you put the time value of money to work for you—compounding your earnings and letting your money make money. The key factor here is time: it takes time for the power of compounding to work for you. Therefore, the sooner you get started with your investing program, the better.

Exercise: Investing and Your Money Script

It is time for you to think again about your money script, as it is this script that may make following the advice in this chapter difficult. If your script is the Power Player, it may be hard to acknowledge that there are things, such as market fluctuations, outside your control. If your script is the Gambler, you may be attracted to the risks of using your investment portfolio as the stake in a dangerous game of chance. If your script is the Masquerader, you may be reluctant to use some of your "keeping up appearances" money for investing in your future.

Take a little time to reflect. Given the self-knowledge that you have been developing, what are the ways you're most likely to sabotage yourself in the area of investing? Imagine that your True Self is gently talking with your money script. Your True Self has a maturity and calm about her, while your money script is more anxious and prone to anxiety and self-sabotage. Your True Self is like a loving parent—understanding your money script but also soothingly setting limits and boundaries for it. When your money script anxiously says that you have to be reactive with money, your True Self gently reminds her that you can make better choices—choices that will enhance your long-term building of wealth. Your True Self tells you to breathe deeply, act calmly, and let your financial actions be informed by wisdom.

This is a situation in which forewarned is forearmed. The more you are consciously aware of the pitfalls you are most susceptible to, the less likely you are to fall into them. Remember that your money script does not reflect your True Self. That Self has wisdom and courage. Allow it to be your guide as you move forward on the path to True Wealth.

Hooray! You've done it. You've completed the most challenging chapter in the book. Don't expect yourself to have absorbed everything you've read. Rather, use this chapter as a reference for when you have specific questions or feel you need a refresher.

> It is better to take many small steps in the right direction than to make a great leap forward only to stumble backward.
> ~ Chinese Proverb

For now, though, let's celebrate your success. Ask yourself, "What would feel good right now?" Maybe you want to call a friend and brag a little about your newfound knowledge. Maybe you'd enjoy a nice meal or a long bath. Whatever sounds good, offer it to yourself. Success is not about self-denial. It's about rejoicing in your progress—giving yourself positive reinforcement for forward movement and recognizing the steps you're taking.

In Summary

Here are the things you need to know to help you succeed in investing:

- Invest automatically each month into your tax-advantaged account.
- Don't try to time when to get into and out of the stock market.
- Be a long-term investor in high-quality, low-expense-ratio mutual funds.
- Set up an asset allocation that fits for your life circumstances.
- Keep your investments diversified.
- Put the time value of money to work for you: get started early and stay invested.

> Don't judge each day by the harvest you reap but by the seeds that you plant.
> ~ **Robert Louis Stevenson, Scottish Writer**

STAYING ON COURSE:
Maintaining Balance
when the Market
Excites Your Emotions

II

Six Pillars of True Wealth
Smart Investing
Home Ownership
Empowered Earning
Conscious Spending and Credit
Adequate Insurance
Wise Planning

> I can calculate the motions of heavenly bodies, but not the madness of people.
> ~ Sir Isaac Newton, after losing over £20,000 in the South Sea Bubble

Smart investing requires intelligence yet that alone is not enough. Intelligence certainly provides no guaranteed protection against investment mistakes. In the early eighteenth century, Sir Isaac Newton, one of the smartest individuals in human history, lost over £20,000 (more than one million dollars in today's currency) in the South Sea Bubble. Jonathan Swift also lost money in the South Sea Bubble, and parodied it in *Gulliver's Travels*, his classic satire of British society. How could men like Newton and Swift, famous for having towering intellects, have been so foolish with their investing? They fell prey to the same trap that ensnared so many of our contemporaries when the tech stock bubble burst in 2000. The investment trap is composed of:

- a contagious excitement about the brave new possibilities for getting rich;
- a herd mentality;
- the belief that the rules of the marketplace have fundamentally changed.

When these factors are combined with a lack of knowledge about the theory of investing, and a lack of understanding about money scripts, they create a formula for catastrophically poor investment choices.

Successful investing requires self-discipline, and self-discipline requires self-awareness. By understanding ourselves better—especially our Achilles heels—we resist the allure of speculative buying when markets heat up. I remember talking with an old friend near the dizzying height of the internet stock bubble. He showed me a glossy financial magazine featuring a picture of a deliriously happy couple holding up handfuls of cash—the headline trumpeted "Everybody's Getting Rich!"

"It's true," my friend asserted. "There's no limit to how much you can make off the stocks of these internet companies. The old rules don't apply to the new economy."

He urged me to invest in a high-tech company that was just going public, assuring me that we would both make a killing. He was certain his stock—a provider of online services—could not miss. He was convinced it was "the new AOL." Despite his enthusiasm, I declined. It turns out that my decision was prudent, since the company he was touting is now in bankruptcy, with its stock value at zero. My friend had invested far too much of his portfolio on this gamble. Like so many others, he got caught up in the financial euphoria of the tech bubble only to have the bubble burst in his face.

> It does not prove a thing to be right because the majority say it is so.
> ~ Friedrich von Schiller, German Dramatist, Poet

Behavioral Finance and Neuroeconomics

Behavioral finance is the academic study of why otherwise sensible people frequently make irrational investment choices. Researchers have discovered some fascinating reasons why people, such as my friend mentioned in the previous paragraph, fall victim to overconfidence in their ill-advised investment choices. One classic mistake is the assumption the recent past will accurately predict the future of an investment's price. For example, during the 1990s tech stock boom, investors disregarded long-term data about many companies' profitability in favor of short-term rises in stock prices. Another investor error that behavioral finance researchers have identified is "overconfidence bias," which means overestimating one's knowledge of a particular investment while underestimating the ability of millions of other investors. A third mistake is known as "anchoring," which is evaluating an asset's worth by its past and current price rather than its intrinsic value. Just as a used car salesman will start the sales pitch by "anchoring" an artificially high price in the customer's mind so that she feels like she's gotten a good deal with a slightly less inflated price, so too investors get "anchored" in past prices that may not reflect the stock's intrinsic value.

> I'd compare stock pickers to astrologers ... but I don't want to bad-mouth astrologers.
> ~ Eugene Fama, Economist

Neuroeconomics is another academic pursuit that is closely related to behavioral finance. Neureconomists not only observe patterns of poor investment decision-making, but they also observe through brain imaging technology the brain activity that occurs during economic decision making. These researchers are engaged in developing a biological model of how we make economic decisions. One helpful insight from neuroeconomics is that we tend to make poor investment choices by basing our decisions on rough, inexact information rather than really gathering the detailed data necessary to evaluate a stock or other investment choice. In experimental situations, people are asked to make economic decisions while their brain is being scanned. Researchers are thereby learning the biology of decision-making. While it may be adaptive from an evolutionary standpoint to make quick decisions based on the information at hand, investment decisions are best made with patience, study, and plenty of data.

Maintaining Discipline During Market Vicissitudes

It is difficult to avoid falling into groupthink when everyone around you is excited by the promise of easy wealth. We are social animals and when those around us seem to be profiting, the human instinct is to jump in. The problem is, of course, that everyone jumping into the stock market at the same time causes the price of stocks to rise to over-inflated heights. After all, the stock market is just like any other market—with lots of demand, prices rise and with reduced demand, prices fall. When the herd gets scared and starts to pull out of the market, overpriced stocks collapse. Investors see their investment money evaporating and start to panic. It is usually this panic that results in the phenomenon of buying high and selling low, a sure road to the poorhouse. The best way to avoid falling prey to herd mentality is:

- to gain insight into your money script as we discussed in chapter 4;
- to learn the philosophy of investing discussed in chapter 10.

With these understandings as a foundation, you will be prepared to deal with the vicissitudes and to become a disciplined, knowledgeable, and successful investor.

Further Insight into Your Money Script

An in-depth understanding of your money script allows you to recognize your vulnerabilities as an investor. It might be hard to understand why anyone would sell stock at the bottom of a market cycle. But let's imagine a worst-case scenario: what if your stocks lost 12.8 percent as the Dow Industrials did on October 29, 1929, or if they lost 22.6

> Most of the time common stocks are subject to irrational and excessive price fluctuations in both directions as the consequences of the ingrained tendency of most people to speculate or gamble . . . to give way to hope, fear, and greed.
> ~ Benjamin Graham, Economist

percent in one day as the Dow did on October 19, 1987?[1] Then it would be easy to feel truly frightened. It is when fear arises that we are most vulnerable to acting out of anxiety from our money scripts, rather than with wisdom and common sense. When you are operating according to your money script but are not consciously aware of it, then the script has enormous power over you. As you gain insight into the script, you begin to reclaim your power and increase your capacity for making conscious choices.

Insight leads to choice. It also leads to emotional resilience. The more you explore your script and unravel the old messages and historical experiences that created it, the more you heal the wounds of the past and become stronger. You develop the ability to be emotionally resilient when other investors are reactive. This emotional resilience is your primary emotional tool in becoming a smart, disciplined investor.

Just because it is easy to participate in the stock market (according to the Investment Policy Institute, more than fifty percent of Americans own mutual funds), does not mean that it is easy to be a successful investor. Successful investing requires an emotional resiliency that belies the idea that investing in the stock market is a simple matter. Emotional reactivity to the market is the enemy of the smart investor. The smart investor is disciplined and willing to tolerate periods of market decline in order to reap the rewards of long-term appreciation. With an understanding of your money script, you will be well-equipped to deal with the market with rational, disciplined, enlightened self-interest.

Let's examine each of the money scripts and explore the characteristic vulnerabilities of each script in both bull and bear markets. Being *aware* of the script can liberate you

> To invest successfully over a lifetime does not require a stratospheric IQ, unusual business insights, or inside information. What's needed is a sound intellectual framework for making decisions and the ability to keep emotions from corroding that framework.
> ~ **Warren Buffett, Investor, Businessman**

---

1 Behr, Peter, and David A. Vise, "Stock Market Suffers Largest Loss in History as Dow Industrial Average Drops 508 Points," *Washington Post*, October 20, 1987, www.washingtonpost.com/wp-srv/business/longterm/blackm/87oct.htm.

from acting it out. This same awareness allows you the freedom to invest wisely.

The Power Player
Vulnerabilities in bull and bear markets

In a bull market, when stock market prices are high, the Power Player feels a need to win in competition with others. He therefore has the vulnerability of joining the investing herd in a bid to be at the head of it.

In a bear market, when stock prices are low, the Power Player is vulnerable to selling low due to his emotional need to compete and win. Buying stocks in a declining market can feel like a "loser."

Pathway to True Wealth

Aware of his desire to dominate others, the Power Player allows himself the deeper awareness that what he really desires is to protect those he loves. He therefore focuses on sound investment strategies that will best protect his family's finances. He learns not to act out his competitive impulses with his investing. Instead, he focuses on long term investing strategies that are in his true self-interest.

The Victim
Vulnerabilities in bull and bear markets

In a bull market, the Victim feels that everybody else is going to make a killing, and he is going to end up on the losing end of the stick. This becomes a self-fulfilling prophecy if he recklessly speculates in high-risk investments.

In a bear market, the Victim feels that he has gotten shorted by the fat-cats on Wall Street and has been done wrong. He is vulnerable to selling low in a self-fulfilling prophecy of his own victimization.

Pathway to True Wealth

Aware of his feelings of victimization, the Victim realizes that he does not need to turn his anger on himself. He therefore makes investment decisions that are well considered and in his own long-term best interests.

The Masquerader
Vulnerabilities in bull and bear markets

In a bull market, the Masquerader needs to feel that he is projecting a successful image. His vulnerability is that he will look to others to confirm his investment decisions. He seeks others' approval and admiration, even if the people he seeks to impress are themselves making poor investment decisions.

In a bear market, the Masquerader feels a need to look good. Embarrassed by falling stock prices, he sells when the market is low, rather than following through with a disciplined strategy.

Pathway to True Wealth

Aware of his need to project an image of financial success, the Masquerader allows himself the deeper awareness that he can feel OK about himself when he takes off his mask. He stays centered in his own True Self, and allows himself the luxury of following his own best investing knowledge rather than trying to impress others.

The Craver
Vulnerabilities in bull and bear markets

In a bull market, the Craver feels like she has not been given her share. She feels left out—like everyone else has been given a fine meal but her. Her vulnerability is that she will impulsively join in the stock-buying spree of the bull market to soothe her feelings of emotional hunger.

In a bear market, the Craver feels stung, as if the market's downturn were directed at her personally. Due to hurt feelings, she sells when prices are low.

Pathway to True Wealth

Aware of her tendency to feel emotionally underfed, the Craver understands that what will fill her up is better connection with the people she loves. She meets her needs for love directly with the people she loves, and is able to avoid acting out her emotional needs with impulsive buying. When the market is down, she avoids impulsive selling.

The Coupon Clipper
Vulnerabilities in bull and bear markets

In a time of overheated stock prices, the Coupon Clipper feels that stocks are too expensive (and she is right!). Her cautious style is a strength during a time when others seem to be throwing caution to the wind.

In a bear market, her vulnerability is that she will miss opportunities to invest due to her overly cautious style. With stocks, as with other things, it is good to buy when the price is low—but the Coupon Clipper often misses opportunity because of her considerable aversion to risk

Pathway to True Wealth

Aware of her tendency to be fear driven and risk aversive, the Coupon Clipper sees that she needs to distinguish between good risk and bad risk. She has learned that good risk allows her to take measured steps toward making her money work for her. Bad risk unnecessarily puts her money in jeopardy. Having learned the theory of investing, she now knows the difference and is able to act rationally in her enlightened self-interest.

The Hoarder
Vulnerabilities in bull and bear markets

In general the Hoarder's defenses tend to be quite adaptive to investing. His orientation is to amassing more and more wealth. He does so in times of bull and bear markets. Hoarders tend to be successful investors. His issue is not so much that his style impedes good investing; instead, the issue is that his hoarding fails to bring him happiness—because money has become a defense against his own emotional vulnerability.

Pathway to True Wealth

The Hoarder becomes aware of his tendency to use the accumulation of money to avoid intimacy and its attendant emotional vulnerability. He learns to use his natural ability to accumulate wealth as a support for a balanced life rather than as a defense against intimacy.

The Procrastinator
Vulnerabilities in bull and bear markets

In an overheated bull market, or in a bear market, the Procrastinator tends to lose out because he is avoiding getting into investments in the first place. By sitting out the market and generally avoiding planning for his financial future, the Procrastinator puts himself and his family at serious risk.

Pathway to True Wealth

Aware of his tendency toward avoidance, the Procrastinator commits to taking charge of his financial life. He invests automatically, by making regular contributions to his retirement accounts into an appropriately allocated portfolio. Now that his investing is automated, he can happily avoid dealing with his accounts, and does not get overly excited in bull markets nor panicky in bear markets; his avoidant nature is now serving him well.

The Prince/Princess
Vulnerabilities in bull and bear markets

In a bull market, when there is much excitement and there are riches to be made in the stock market, the Prince feels a sense of entitlement. He feels that he should be getting his share of the riches that others seem to be obtaining. He is vulnerable to speculative buying from the emotional vantage point of an excessive sense of entitlement.

In a bear market, the Prince is again vulnerable. His sense of entitlement is rocked by the losses he has experienced. Rather than hanging tight for the long run, he is vulnerable to selling low due to his hurt pride and his anger at a stock market that is indifferent to him.

Pathway to True Wealth

Aware of his inflated sense of entitlement, the Prince has learned that financial markets are quite impersonal and feel no special obligation to any individual. He learns to use his natural sense of entitlement in his own self-interest. Now he feels entitled to the long-term gains that derive from a diversified portfolio rather than feeling that he is entitled to fabulous, unrealistic returns from his portfolio.

The Gambler
Vulnerabilities in bull and bear markets

The Gambler is the most vulnerable to both buying high in bull markets and selling low in bear markets of all of the money types. In an overheated bull market, the Gambler wants in. Investing, for him, is a rush. He does not want to watch others win in the investing game while he sits it out. He is quite drawn to speculative investments. In a bear market, the Gambler is also vulnerable. Having lost value in his investments, he feels it is time to fold. He sells when the market is at the low point with a Gambler's sense of having lost.

Pathway to True Wealth

Aware of his tendency to treat the stock market like a roulette wheel rather than as a long-term place to invest, the Gambler turns his passions elsewhere. He learns that the quickest way to go broke is try to beat the odds. Instead, he learns the art and science of proper asset allocation and long-term investing. He learns to get his kicks elsewhere and to use his investing only for investments.

The Co-Dependent
Vulnerabilities in bull and bear markets

The Co-Dependent is often the spouse of the Gambler. She is more interested in keeping her husband satisfied in his unwise investing schemes than she is in protecting herself and her family financially. In both bull and bear markets, she is focused only on her husband and his moods. She does not pay attention to what is happening in the market because of her focus on her husband. She shirks her financial responsibility to her family with her focus on keeping her husband happy.

Pathway to True Wealth

The Co-Dependent becomes aware of her tendency to focus on keeping her husband happy, even while he is acting out with the family's money in ways that may be quite damaging. She turns her unhealthy co-dependence into healthy financial self-care. She focuses on herself and her family and learns to assert herself with her husband. She confronts him when he wants to buy high and sell low. She learns the theory of investing, and learns how to assert her point of view in the family's financial decisions.

Investing in the stock market is nothing like putting your money in the bank. If you invest in stocks, your emotions will be stirred during periods of volatility, whether the market is up or down. You will be tempted to buy high when everyone seems to be getting rich in a bull market, and you will be tempted to sell low when everyone seems to be losing their shirts in a bear market. Informed investors have learned to avoid the emotional traps that lead to buying high and selling low. They achieve this by understanding their money script, by knowing the history of the stock market, and by understanding investing theory.

Informed investors choose to invest in stocks and to endure the ups and downs of the stock market because of the rewards that have historically been possible in the stock market. Informed investors know that from 1926 through 2004, stocks have produced a healthy average annual return of 10.4 percent. On the other hand, they also know that in individual years during the past thirty years, returns have ranged from −26.5 percent (in 1974) to +37.4 percent (in 1995). They know that stocks have historically behaved with volatility in the short term and growth in the long term.

Informed investors did not sell their stock portfolios when the market was down by 26.5 percent in 1974. Instead, they understood that although such losses are emotionally wrenching, the market, in the long run, will reflect the underlying value of the stocks they own. Similarly, when the market was up 37.4 percent in 1995, informed investors did not speculate on stocks they felt they could make a quick killing on (only to lose their shirts when the bubble burst). They maintained their emotional equilibrium and a balanced mix of stocks, bonds, cash, and other securities even

> You get recessions, you have stock market declines. If you don't understand that's going to happen, then you're not ready, you won't do well in the markets.
> ~ Peter Lynch, Mutual Fund Manager

while their neighbors and friends were betting everything on the latest technology stock.

Becoming a smart investor requires three areas of knowledge:

1. A basic knowledge of the theory of investing
2. A general knowledge of stock market history so as to understand market behavior
3. The self-knowledge that comes with understanding your money script

With this knowledge in hand, you have the perspective, understanding, and emotional resiliency to succeed as an investor. You have the tools to be a first-rate steward of your family's financial resources.

In the short term, the stock market is a voting machine, but in the long term it is a weighing machine.

~ Warren Buffett

HOME OWNERSHIP:
Build Home Equity

Six Pillars of True Wealth
Smart Investing
Home Ownership
Empowered Earning
Conscious Spending and Credit
Adequate Insurance
Wise Planning

> When we boost the number of homeowners in our country, we strengthen our economy, create jobs, build up the middle class, and build better citizens.
> ~ **Bill Clinton**

The second pillar of your financial success is the equity you own in your home. Why is this so important? Owning your home does more than simply provide you with a comfortable place to live. For most people, their home is their most valuable asset. Rising real estate prices throughout the United States over the last fifty years have turned home equity into a source of wealth for many Americans. The greater your equity—that is, the less your mortgage in relation to the market value of the home—the greater the asset. Buying a home and continuing to build equity in it are indispensable steps in creating True Wealth. With forethought, you may be able to coordinate the payoff of your mortgage with your retirement. This will relieve you of your mortgage payment—a major expense—after you are no longer working.

Why You Should Own Your Own Home

Tax advantages

Homeowners have many financial advantages over renters. For one, federal government policy encourages home ownership. Legislators of all political stripes agree that home ownership is good for families and promotes economic stability and good citizenship. The most significant tax advantage is the mortgage interest deduction. In the first years of a standard thirty-year mortgage, most of the payment goes toward interest. Let's say, for example, that you have a thirty-year mortgage at 6.5 percent. In the first year, your monthly payments would total $25,754, of which $19,292 would go toward interest. Your mortgage interest would be deductible, thereby lowering your taxable income by $19,292—quite a reduction!

The tax advantages of home ownership do not stop there. You may also be able to deduct part of the "points" you have paid to the lender in closing costs on your mortgage. Additionally, you may deduct property taxes you have paid on your home. You can easily see that home ownership has a truly significant impact in tax savings alone.

Forced savings

Another advantage of home ownership is that it is a means of automatic saving. With a traditional loan, a portion of your monthly mortgage payment goes toward reducing the principal. As you reduce your principal, you are automatically building equity—ownership—in your home. You are investing in your house, and if your house appreciates in value (as has historically been the case), then your investment has appreciated in value.

Sound Investments vs. Speculative Investments

With real estate it is easy to confuse investment with speculation, so we want to clarify the difference. You are making a sound investment when you purchase an asset that has

The strength of a nation derives from the integrity of the home.

~ Confucius

intrinsic value (such as a house) with the plan to build ownership or equity in the investment. A speculative investment, on the other hand, is one bought with the hope that you'll be able to find a buyer at a higher price. This is a critical difference.

It is a sound investment to buy a home that you can afford with a traditional thirty-year mortgage. It is a speculative investment to buy a house that is beyond your means with an interest-only adjustable interest rate loan that will come due in five years, hoping to make a profit on it before the five years are up. To put it another way, a sound investment builds equity in an asset with intrinsic value; a speculative investment is a bet that the next guy will pay more just because you think he will.

> A house can have integrity, just like a person.
> ~ Ayn Rand

Unless you are wealthy and can speculate with money that is non-essential for you, you should not be a speculative investor. With your home, especially, it is important to be a sound investor. It is a widely held myth that real estate prices only go up. In reality that is not the case. Like any asset class, real estate values have good years and bad years, so buy your own home and build equity in that home by paying down the principal. For this reason we strongly advise against interest-only loans. Just as the name implies, an interest-only loan does not help you build equity.

With an interest-only loan, you will owe the lending company the same amount that you owed when you took out the loan. For example, if you were to get a ten-year interest-only loan on $350,000, make your mortgage payments diligently, and sell the house in ten years, your payoff amount will still be the original $350,000. This could make life unpleasant if you should need to sell when housing prices are down. You could find yourself having to pay the difference between the sale amount for the house and the original loan amount out-of-pocket.

There are some unusual circumstances when an interest-only loan can be a good choice, but as a general rule you should not be fooled by the appearance of building owner-ship with interest-only loans and other creative financing. Instead, focus on paying down your mortgage as soon as possible so that you, not the bank, are the owner of your house.

Pay Down Your Mortgage Early

Now that we have (hopefully) convinced you to purchase a traditional mortgage, which allows you to build equity, let's go one step further. If you want move more quickly toward True Wealth, a great tool is to *pay down your mortgage early*! We suggest that you add an additional 15 percent to each and every mort-gage payment you make to the bank. For example if you had a $300,000 loan with a thirty-year mortgage at 6.5 percent, your monthly payment would come to approximately $1,896. If you add 15 percent ($284) to that payment each month, and that payment goes to paying down your princi-pal, then you would save more than $129,000 over the course of the mortgage and own your home outright almost nine years sooner. That is a good investment!

You can find some great tools on our website to calculate your potential savings by prepaying your mortgage. At *www.insightfinancialgroup.com*, go to the Calculators link, then to Consumer Debt, and finally to the Loan Acceleration calcu-lator. If adding 15 percent to the monthly payment is too much of a bite, try adding 10 percent. Have fun with the 0calculator and see how much you can save with this simple but effective technique.

Think Like the Bank

There is a fundamental difference in the way banks think about home loans and the way consumers look at them. Banks look at how much money they will make over the course of the loan, whereas consumers look at how big their payment will be each month. Here, then, is a valuable tip as you move toward True Wealth: think like the bank! Instead

> These [variable rate mortgage] products could be cause for some concern both because they expose borrowers to more interest-rate and house-price risk than the standard thirty-year, fixed-rate mortgage.
> ~ **Alan Greenspan, Economist, Chairman of the Federal Reserve**

of focusing on how minimal a payment you can make each month, consider how much you are going to be paying over time. Creative financing (using tools such as interest-only loans) may make your monthly payments low, but they do nothing to help you pay off the loan over time. No wonder banks love these loans. They allow the banks to get payments from the consumer without offering equity in return. We suggest you tip the scales in your own favor: make life a little more difficult for the bank, and a little better for you, by paying a larger sum each month and saving yourself money in the long run.

> For the typical family, home equity accounts for the bulk of their wealth.
> ~ **Frank Nothaft,**
> **Economist**

Exercise: Defining Home

Take some time to contemplate the following questions. You may want to write or draw your responses in your Money Journal. These questions may also stimulate a discussion between you and your partner or a family member:

• When you hear the word "home," what images come to mind?
• What makes a house a home?
• How does feeling "at home" support you in your life and work?
• How might you stop yourself from providing a comfortable, secure home for yourself?
• What sort of support do you need in order to take the steps toward establishing a comfortable, secure home?

In Summary

Owning your own home is the third pillar of your financial success. Keep the following tips in mind, and you'll be well on your way to building this necessary foundation for True Wealth:

· As a home owner, you'll reap the benefits of the home mortgage interest deduction come tax time.
· Owning your home with a traditional mortgage forces you to save money by building equity in the house.

- Unless you're very wealthy, buy a house that's a sound investment, not a speculative one.
- If you can, add 10 to 15 percent to your mortgage payment each month to save money over the life of the mortgage.
- Paying down your mortgage early will save you many thousands of dollars in the long run.

To be happy at home is the ultimate result of all ambition.
~ Samuel Johnson, Poet

EMPOWERED EARNING

13

Six Pillars of True Wealth
Smart Investing
Home Ownership
Empowered Earning
Conscious Spending and Credit
Adequate Insurance
Wise Planning

> And as we let our own light shine, we unconsciously give other people permission to do the same. As we are liberated from our fear, our presence automatically liberates others.
> ~ Marianne Williamson, Author

What are you worth? In the eyes of God, of course, we all have infinite value. To our families and loved ones, we are priceless. Our contributions to the greater good of our communities and the world can have lasting significance. There is another aspect to this question, however, that is important to address as you move toward True Wealth: What is your "market value"? Are you receiving an equitable reward for your time and skills?

One step on the Buddhist Eightfold Path is Right Livelihood, which includes treating others *and yourself* with fairness. Let's explore two aspects of Right Livelihood: (1) acknowledging your true gifts and offering them to the world, and (2) receiving fair compensation for those gifts. To do these two things requires faith in yourself and a sense that the world can meet you with abundance.

There is a subtle but powerful interplay between how you perceive yourself and the opportunities that manifest for you in your life. In this chapter, we give you the tools to begin the transformation of the feedback loop between how you perceive yourself and the abundance that you experience.

We have seen throughout this book that working with our Economic Self offers us an unparalleled opportunity to increase our self-support and to value our own worth. Let's take a moment to explore the meaning of self-support and look at how it differs from selfishness. Self-support is the capacity to honor what we feel and think and to respond to our own needs. Many of us have been taught to believe that doing this is selfish or self-centered. However, there is an important distinction between real self-support and mere selfishness. The selfish person values his or her needs above those of others; he promotes himself at the expense of others. A self-supporting person looks for ways to bring his or her own special contribution into the world. A self-supporting stance is one that promotes the well-being of yourself and others at the same time. Where selfishness takes away from others, self-support adds to others' well-being.

From a spiritual perspective, it is important to recognize that you have a vital part to play in the great symphony of life. Kabbalists tell us that God and humanity are co-creating the universe. The universe is depending on you to play your part to your fullest. Kabbalah teaches that when you do so, you help send healing sparks into the universe, and are doing your part to heal not only yourself but the universe. When you show up more fully in your work, expressing your own true self in that work and valuing yourself enough to expect a fair reward for the work, you are showing up more fully in the universe. You are playing the role that is yours and yours alone.

> Be not afraid of growing slowly, be afraid only of standing still.
> ~ **Chinese Proverb**

Exercise: Work and Earning

Let's get focused on your work and your earning. Start a section in your Money Journal called Work and Earning. Here are some questions to ask yourself:

- What are you happy with about your work?
- What would you like to change about your work?
- How are you expressing your talents in your work?
- How could you more fully express your talents?

Don't censor yourself as you respond to these questions. Write or draw whatever comes to mind, without judgment. Keep these responses in mind as you read the rest of the chapter.

> Don't compromise yourself. You are all you've got.
> ~ Janis Joplin

The Negative Feedback Loop

As we've mentioned, your money script is a leftover from childhood that limits the ways you think about yourself and your self-worth. As you move past your money script into money empowerment, you learn to value yourself, to expect that you will be well-compensated for what you do. The trick here is to recognize the negative feedback loop that can reinforce a limiting script. The negative feedback loop looks something like this: Your money script emits a self-limiting message to the world. People come to know you in this limited way. You are put in a limited role in your work. You get comfortable there. Others get comfortable seeing you there. Now you are really stuck! You are playing a limited role, which is reinforced by your money script, the way others see you, and the fact that you get comfortable there. No wonder change is so challenging. Let's look at an example.

Florence is one of our financial planning clients. She has an accounting degree from a prestigious university, and her money script is the Coupon Clipper.

Growing up in a small town, she had an alcoholic father who worked as a handyman. Her mom waited tables.

Florence lacked basic security in her childhood, not just economically but also emotionally. Her dad was often drunk, and her mom was depressed and frequently exhausted from her waitressing job.

Florence is very smart. A top student in high school, she received a full scholarship to college where she majored in accounting. Poised to begin her career with a top degree and bankable skills, her Coupon Clipper money script kicked in just as she began her first job.

Although prestigious accounting firms regularly interviewed accounting majors at her college, Florence never felt confident enough to attend the interviews. Instead, she chose to begin her career in the role of bookkeeper at a small business, with a small salary. Her conscious reasoning was that this job would be a comfortable place to begin her career. Underneath the conscious reasoning, however, the Coupon Clipper money script lurked with its fear base. Florence was carrying an emotional load from childhood that did not make space for her to support her own financial needs in a healthy manner. Within the script of the Coupon Clipper, she felt safer with limited work responsibilities and limited pay. People at the job soon forgot about her prestigious degree and came to see her as she saw herself—an assistant bookkeeper. People with far fewer skills and intelligence were promoted ahead of her. Florence was frustrated that people saw her in this way, but she did not yet recognize how she had contributed to this state of affairs.

When our financial planning work began, we identified her money script as the Coupon Clipper. Florence came to see how fear, brought on by the lack of security she had felt in childhood, had ruled her life. We worked on helping her expand out of the old and tired money script and into her empowered Economic Self. She began to articulate the kind of work that she really wanted and felt qualified for: the position of comptroller at a medium-size company.

People wish to swim and at the same time to keep one foot on the ground.
~ Marcel Proust

Pushing past her old, fear-based money script was not easy, but Florence gathered her courage and started applying for the kind of work she was qualified for. She landed an assistant-comptroller position with a fast-growing company. After two successful years, her boss moved on to a new job, and she was promoted to the comptroller job. Florence is now making five times what she was making in her bookkeeping position. Even more important, she is much happier and feels a great deal better about herself. She is a terrific supervisor and mentor to people in her department and has helped her firm flourish in ways that she never could have while trapped in her old money script.

The first step in undoing the negative feedback loop is to become aware of it. The negative feedback loop can be so self-reinforcing that it is hard to see. Let's start with an exercise in your Money Journal to help you get a handle on any negative feedback loop that may be occurring in your work life.

> Creativity involves breaking out of established patterns in order to look at things in a different way.
> ~ Edward De Bono, Writer

Exercise: Exploring the Negative Feedback Loop
Ask yourself the following questions:

- What is your money script? (See chapter 4 to revisit the different kinds.)
- Has your money script created a self-limiting message that you put out into the world?
- Have people at your work come to know you in a limited way?
- Is your role at work out of sync with your skills and passion?
- Have you become complacent and comfortable with a limited vision of yourself?

By becoming aware of any ways that you contribute to a self-limiting negative feedback loop, you can start to create change and put yourself on more positive footing.

The Positive Feedback Loop
Now let's turn our attention to the positive! The positive feedback loop looks something like this: working through

the money script, you put out a self-confident message to the world. People in the work world come to know the self-confident you. You are given responsibility, status, and money in your work. You get comfortable there. Others get comfortable seeing you there. The positive feedback loop creates confidence, connection with others, and prosperity.

In order to think about what you would like to do with your work to make more money and to express your talents more fully, let's start with an exercise.

Exercise: Your Ideal Work Life

Allow your body to relax, and settle into your chair or cushion. Gently turn your attention to your breath, feeling your lungs fill and empty. We are now going to work with a breathing exercise from the Sufi tradition.

The breath of air (one of the five purification breaths) is done by breathing in and out through the mouth. Slightly purse your lips as if breathing through a straw. On the inhale, imagine all the energy of the universe flowing into you with no effort on your part. On the exhale, allow any negative self-image to flow out and be dissolved into the greater whole. Visualize the color blue, like the blue of a clear sky. After at least five inhalations/exhalations, allow your breathing to return to normal, and sit quietly for a few moments, feeling the effects of this practice.

You will be aware of a sense of openness and expansiveness. You are allowing your synapses, the very molecules in your brain, to expand and allow new creative space. You are, in a sense, "plugging in" to the universal energy source. This source is limitless and always available if you open yourself to it. It is only when you shut down and narrow your focus that you lose touch with your own vastness and infinite potential.

From this place of expansiveness, begin to think about your work life. Allow yourself to envision an ideal scenario:

- What would an ideal day at work look like?
- Where would you be working?
- Who would you be working with?
- How much would you be paid?
- How would you feel at the end of the work day?

> Everyone has inside of him a piece of good news. The good news is that you don't know how great you can be! How much you can love! What you can accomplish! And what your potential is!
> ~ Anne Frank

Take a moment to jot down your answers to these questions in your Money Journal. What feelings come up as you look over your answers? Are you excited? Curious? Nervous? Whatever the feelings, just experience them to the fullest. Paying attention to and honoring your feelings is one part of making the changes that will lead to increased fulfillment in your work.

Exercise: Your Five-Year Plan

The other part of making changes is more intellectual. In a new section of your Money Journal, create a page titled "My Five-Year Plan." Under this heading write the answers to the following questions:

> You see things, and you say "Why?" but I dream things that never were, and I say "Why not?"
> ~ George Bernard Shaw, Writer

- What would you like to be doing in the work world in five years? Make the answer to this question as specific and detailed as possible. For instance, instead of answering "I'd like to be a manager," say "I'd like to be managing the copywriting department of the company where I am now. I would have six employees working under me and be making double my current salary."
- What would need to happen for you to reach your goal? For instance, "I'd need to make a great impression on the advertising director. I need to find ways to let him see my talent firsthand. I'd also need to improve my supervisory skills."
- What can you do over the next six months to begin moving toward your goal? For instance, "I can take a course in effective management. I can speak up more often in departmental meetings and offer my suggestions rather than letting shyness inhibit me."

Over the next six months, begin to implement your plan. Commit to having monthly meetings with yourself in which you review your goal, assess your progress, and refine your plan. It can be especially helpful to share this process with a partner, friend, or coach. Look for someone who will encourage you when you get discouraged, cheer your accomplishments, and keep you honest as you move toward the success you deserve.

Empowering your earning is a basic building block in creating wealth; more money earned can lead to more money invested in your future. The benefits of empowering your earning go way beyond just increasing your bottom line, however; these benefits go right to the heart of building True Wealth. When you empower your earning, you are learning to value your own worth and to assert your value in the workplace. As you grow in this process, you come to see yourself in a new light, and others come to see you in that new light as well. You bring the best of yourself into the world, not only for your own benefit but for the benefit of everyone you work with.

The secret of success is consistency of purpose.
~ Benjamin Disraeli,
   Former British Prime
   Minister

SPENDING:
You Can Never Get Enough of the Wrong Thing— A Woman's Perspective

Six Pillars of True Wealth
Smart Investing
Home Ownership
Empowered Earning
Conscious Spending and Credit
Adequate Insurance
Wise Planning

> The odds of going to the store for a loaf of bread and coming out with ONLY a loaf of bread are three billion to one.
> ~ Erma Bombeck, Humorist, Columnist

Many years ago, in my (Daisy's) single days, I saw a personal ad under "Men Seeking Women" that read, in part: "Believe it or not, I *love* to shop. If that's one of your favorite pastimes, give me a call and LET'S GO SHOPPING." At first I laughed, but I couldn't deny my fascination. Finally I contacted the guy. He told me that he had been absolutely inundated with calls from women of all ages. He could hardly believe his good fortune! Although I never actually met this man, the memory of his ad has stayed with me. Apparently he had, unwittingly, tapped into an aspect of female psychology that can wreak havoc in women's lives.

Certainly, it's not only women who can be bitten by the shopping bug. Studies show that men are the ones more likely to overspend on high-tech gadgets. ("He who dies with the most toys wins.") Cars are a primary male status symbol and much automobile advertising is clearly aimed at men. For many reasons, however, it seems that women are more susceptible to the many enticements our culture offers to shop and spend.

"Shop till you drop." "When the going gets tough, the tough go shopping." These are the messages that bombard women daily. We see them on billboards, read them in magazines, hear the jingles sung on radio and television. We are definitely saturated with the sales pitch. Some companies even provide free equipment to schools in exchange for being allowed to advertise to the students, a captive audience.

Saturation is part of the answer to the question of why we overspend, but part of the answer is more internal. Let's take a look at three of the basic internal messages that underlie habitual overspending:

> I take Him shopping with me. I say, OK, Jesus, help me find a bargain.
>
> ~ Tammy Faye Bakker Messner

Spending as Self-Soothing

"I can't have what I really want,
so I'll try to satisfy myself with material goods."

I'm willing to bet that most of us have at least occasionally resorted to spending as a means of self-soothing. Do you remember your last romantic breakup? Chances are that you dealt with the loss of a love by either over-eating or over-spending. If you're like me, you may have managed to do both at once—shopping for over-priced gourmet items and then feasting! If spending in this way is merely an occasional blip on your radar screen, there's probably no need to worry. However, if you find yourself frequently at the mall for no purpose other than "just shopping," it's time for some self-examination.

Working with your money script can help you gain a better understanding of how and why you may be using over-spending to self-soothe. The money scripts which would make you most susceptible to spending as self-soothing are the Craver and the Victim. Let's see how this can play out.

Sylvia's money script was the Craver. Her childhood had been a most unusual one. Her parents had come of age in the sixties and had taken very literally the message to "turn on, tune in, and drop out." They became committed to the "back to the land" and "voluntary simplicity" movements. By the time Sylvia was two, she and her brother were living with their parents on a farm in rural Vermont. Sylvia's father built the family's cabin with the help of neighbors and struggled to grow their food in the rocky soil. Her mother made the children's clothes and spent most of each summer canning and preserving food for the coming winter. The children were home schooled and expected to do their part in keeping the family going.

Sylvia and her brother were greatly loved and well-cared for. As children they never went hungry or lacked for basic necessities. Any request for a special toy or a fashionable outfit, however, was frowned upon as an indication that the children were being infected by culture's mass media and commercialism. Sylvia's parents sincerely believed that they were protecting their children from the ill effects of a materialistic society. Unfortunately, their approach created in Sylvia a seemingly insatiable desire for the things she had been denied as a child. Now in her thirties and a successful MBA, Sylvia has learned to soothe her feelings by spending money. Her career has kept her too busy to have much of a romantic life and her isolated childhood has made her a little awkward and hesitant in social situations. Sylvia spends many an evening browsing through her plethora of catalogs and ordering anything that strikes her fancy. She is momentarily satisfied, but when the items arrive they are never quite right. Since what she is actually longing for can't be found in a catalog, Sylvia is left feeling disappointed and depleted. These feelings lead her to still more spending, and the cycle continues.

Barbara, Sylvia's executive assistant, is different from her boss in many ways, but she too is caught in the trap of spending to self-soothe. Unlike Sylvia's family, Barbara's

> Craving, not having, is the mother of a reckless giving of oneself.
> ~ Eric Hoffer, Writer

family lived simply by necessity rather than choice. As the oldest of seven siblings, Barbara was expected to be her mother's right hand. She came straight home from school each day in order to help with the housekeeping and cooking. She learned at an early age that the quickest way to gain approval from her mother was to be generous with her younger brothers and sisters. She began babysitting for the neighbors at age twelve and spent most of her earnings buying treats for the little ones. Once she became an adult, Barbara continued her same pattern of selflessness.

She has helped put several of her siblings through college and now is supporting her husband as he earns his law degree. Although she longs to return to school herself, she sees this as only a fantasy. Barbara is less interested than Sylvia in catalogs; she spends every weekend at her local mall. Most frequently, her purchases are for others. Somehow, she seems to end many of her shopping trips feeling angry and depressed. Rather than exploring these feelings, she deals with them by increasing her spending, and the cycle continues.

Do you, like Sylvia and Barbara, spend to self-soothe? Ask yourself a few questions:

- When I feel sad, mad, or lonely, do I try to avoid the feeling by shopping?
- Do I often find myself shopping with nothing particular in mind, "just to pass the time"?
- Am I often surprised by the credit card bills at the end of the month?
- Do I frequently look at recent purchases and wonder, "What in the world was I thinking?"
- Do I sometimes emerge from a shopping experience feeling like I've just awakened from a dream?

If you answered yes to many or all of these questions, you may find the following exercises helpful.

> Twenty million Americans are only one paycheck ahead of catastrophe. Their debts are destroying them.
>
> ~ **Luther Gatling, President of Budget and Credit Counseling Service**

Exercise: Repeating Question

You can do this exercise either with a partner or on your own, whichever your prefer. If you are working with a partner, your partner should ask the first question, wait for your response, and say "thank you." Then your partner should ask the same question again. If you are working on your own, simply ask yourself the question, take a few moments, and then respond to the question.

Whether you are working on your own or with a partner, the point is to explore your responses with no judgments. Do not comment on the responses or change the questions. Instead, simply witness your responses. This is a "spoken meditation." The question is like the flame that the meditator stares into—it doesn't change, but the meditator's perception deepens.

Once a five-minute period is over, go quietly to your Money Journal and record whatever thoughts and feelings the exercise has stirred in you. Work with only one question at a time. Let at least a few hours elapse before working with the second question. Here are the questions:

> It is preoccupation with possessions, more than anything else, that prevents us from living freely and nobly.
> ~ Bertrand Russell,
> Writer, Philosopher

- What is it you really want?
- How do you stop yourself from getting what you really want?

If you work with this exercise over time, you will find that your answers to the questions grow deeper and richer. You will begin to discover parts of yourself that you've been only dimly aware of. You will begin to step free from the cycle of spending to self-soothe by acknowledging your true feelings and addressing your true needs.

Spending to Relieve Anxiety

> *"There's something 'wrong' or inadequate about me.*
> *Maybe I can fix it with my next purchase."*

Is your breath fresh enough? Is your hair shiny? Do you see signs of premature aging? Does your home exude warmth and welcome? Are your children wearing the right clothes to fit in with the popular crowd? If you felt a tiny shiver of anxiety while reading over those questions, welcome to modern Western culture. It's hard to avoid being affected by

Madison Avenue's carefully calculated program to convince us that we "need" more and more. For some of us, though, the external pressure to spend in order to feel OK about ourselves coincides with an internal pressure to do the same. The money scripts that make people especially susceptible to this type of spending are the Masquerader and the Co-Dependent. Consider the following example.

Lois learned early to follow a Masquerader script. Her family was comfortably middle-class, but her parents had grand ambitions. They cut corners on many things in order to send Lois to the town's most exclusive private school. There, they reasoned, she would mingle with the daughters of the wealthy and powerful and be ready to live the kind of life they could only dream of. Unfortunately, Lois's parents didn't realize that paying the tuition at the private school would be the least of the demands on their finances. Lois found herself in class with girls whose monthly allowance was the same as her father's monthly paycheck. Weekends at ski chalets, shopping trips to New York, and summers in Europe were commonplace.

Lois quickly recognized that she had no way of keeping up with her classmates. Being resourceful and imaginative, she learned to create an illusion of wealth that she was far from possessing. When she was invited on trips she couldn't afford, Lois excused herself by saying things like, "I'd love to go, but my dad's promised to take us on a photo safari in Kenya." Then she would comb the internet to find and print pictures to show at school when she "returned." Lois spent all of her allowance and babysitting money on designer clothes from consignment boutiques. She lived in terror that one of her classmates would see her in one of their discarded outfits.

Because Lois was pretty and charming, her masquerade was never questioned and she carried the script into adulthood. Today she is constantly overextended financially. It's vitally important to her to have the latest fashions and to

> Too many people spend money they haven't earned, to buy things they don't want, to impress people they don't like.
> ~ Will Rogers, Humorist

drive a late-model luxury car. Ironically, she works at an advertising agency, where she spends her days stimulating the anxieties of others in the name of marketing.

Geraldine is caught in the trap of the Co-Dependent script. When she overspends, it is most often on behalf of her children. Growing up with an alcoholic father left Geraldine with a chronic feeling of anxiety. She learned early to be a "fixer," and spending money is the way she often tries to fix a problem.

She has always wanted her children to have the best and has worked hard to provide it for them. She hasn't wanted them to grow up like her father—bitter and drinking to alleviate his disappointment in life—or like herself—constantly running just to stay in the same place. When her children get into trouble, Geraldine rushes in immediately. Her husband admonishes her that "you can't fix a problem by throwing money at it," and Geraldine nods in agreement. Her anxiety feels so overwhelming, however, that she often can't control her impulse. When her son was laid off recently, Geraldine was right there, offering to cover his mortgage payments until he found another job. Her husband is looking toward retirement and worries that Geraldine's spending will disrupt his plans. She is beginning to recognize that she has a significant problem but feels lost about how to work with it.

Here are some questions to ask yourself to determine whether you, like Lois and Geraldine, spend to relieve anxiety:

- Do I ever feel pressure to buy "something," even though I'm not sure what?
- Do I find myself buying and discarding cosmetics, clothes, or household items in a search of "just the right thing"?
- Do I sometimes feel that if I could only find the right shampoo, lipstick, and so on. I could relax?

> Shopping is a woman thing. It's a contact sport like football. Women enjoy the scrimmage, the noisy crowds, the danger of being trampled to death, and the ecstasy of the purchase.
> ~ **Erma Bombeck, Humorist, Columnist**

- Do I think that many, if not most, problems can be solved with money?
- Do I believe that there are certain things my children must have in order to become successful adults?

If you feel that you are caught up in spending to relieve anxiety, there is really only one road out of the vicious cycle you're caught in. The task ahead of you is to develop an emotional "container" that's large enough to hold your anxiety. The emotional container relates to your ability to tolerate your feelings and not act out on them. There is a big difference between suppressing your feelings and containing them. To suppress your feelings is to fail to acknowledge them even to yourself, sometimes not even allowing them to come to conscious awareness. Containing your feelings acknowledges them but also allows you to choose consciously how you want to act in response to the feelings. This is far better than acting out in unmindful ways just to relieve your anxiety.

Once you become better at containing your feelings, you will feel less of a need to act them out. Depending on how deeply entrenched your pattern of anxious spending is, you may need some sessions with a professional therapist to resolve the issue. Before you seek out professional help, however, here are some techniques to work with on your own:

- Meditation is a powerful tool for calming anxiety and easing stress. A basic meditation technique is to simply sit quietly with your eyes closed and pay attention to your breath. You can count your breaths or practice inhaling for four counts, waiting four counts, and then exhaling for four counts. If you practice this for a few minutes each day, you will develop a resource to use whenever you start to feel the familiar push to spend. Make a deal with yourself that whenever you

> If we know the divine art of concentration, if we know the divine art of meditation, if we know the divine art of contemplation, easily and consciously we can unite the inner world and the outer world.
>
> ~ Sri Chinmoy,
>   Philosopher, Teacher

feel inclined to spend money on an "extra," you will take a ten-minute time-out to sit quietly and breathe consciously.

- Twelve-step groups have evolved a number of catchy and helpful mantras. One that can be especially useful for anxious spenders is H.A.L.T. If you are feeling Hungry, Angry, Lonely, or Tired, HALT—otherwise you will be vulnerable to impulsive behavior that will leave you feeling regretful. You may also recognize other triggers for yourself. Work on becoming increasingly aware of these triggers, and learn to respond to them in ways other than overspending.

- Finding a sponsor is another helpful contribution from twelve-step groups. Having a trusted friend to whom you can reach out when you're feeling vulnerable is invaluable. Make it a goal to develop at least one of these friendships, and practice asking for and accepting support.

- It is a true that "the best things in life are free." Start a list of the blessings in your life that aren't related to money. The more you pay attention to and cultivate these aspects of your life, the less compulsive you'll feel about spending.

> When we spend despite a decision or desire not to, or spend to our own detriment, we are spending compulsively.
> ~ **Debtors Anonymous**

Spending to Belong

"I'm in search of community. I need a way to define myself."

Belonging—feeling a part of a group—is a natural human need. We all wish to be liked and respected, to feel accepted and valued. Unfortunately, our consumer culture exploits this human need for marketing purposes. Whether you're a teenager who *has* to have Nikes because "that's what everybody's wearing," a young mother who *has* to provide her child with a brand new bike because "that's what all the fourth graders are getting for Christmas this year," or a rising executive who *has* to buy a house in the most expensive suburb because "that's what people in my position do," the chances are good that you've been (at least occasionally) caught in the "spend to belong" trap.

Whatever your money script, spending to belong can be seductive. Since it is so pervasive and culturally approved, how can you combat it? Let's consider some steps you can take to make yourself less susceptible to this kind of overspending.

> Compulsive shopping leads to serious psychological, financial, and family problems, including depression, overwhelming debt, and the breakup of relationship.
> ~ **Dr. Lorrin Koran,**
> **Stanford University**

- Educate yourself and your children. The more you're aware of advertisers' tricks to convince you to buy what you don't need, the less you'll be vulnerable to them.
- If your children watch television, spend a little time each week watching with them. Analyze the commercials. Talk together about the ways in which the media speak to our anxieties and longings, and implicitly promise something unobtainable.
- Become a savvy consumer. Consult a guide such as Consumer Reports before making major purchases. Comparison shop rather than buying on impulse.
- Explore the voluntary simplicity movement. Get to know other people who are working to simplify their lives, and avoid conspicuous consumption.
- Experiment with ways to enjoy yourself without emphasizing spending money. How would it be to celebrate Christmas with only homemade gifts? What about a homestay rather than a vacation at an expensive resort?
- Think about how real community is developed. Can you connect with your neighbors? Are there volunteer organizations where your contribution would bring you satisfaction and a wider network? Could you and your friends start some sort of cooperative venture— for instance, a babysitting co-op or a community garden?

Once you begin to work toward what you actually want—a sense of belonging and community—you'll find yourself connecting with like-minded people. You'll be developing True Wealth, which doesn't depend simply on the amount of your bank balance. Your life will become richer and more authentic. You can't get enough of what you don't really need, but you'll find that you can get enough of what truly satisfies. What truly satisfies are relationships that money can't buy.

The best things in life aren't things.

~ **Art Buchwald,**
Columnist

CREDIT AND DEBT ISSUES:
Spending Consciously and Wisely

15

Backpackers have an apt saying: "Take care of the ounces, and the pounds will take care of themselves." So it goes in our financial lives: take care of the dollars, and the thousands will take care of themselves. Saving dollars leads to saving thousands of dollars. We invest those thousands wisely, and before long, we have accumulated real money.

Staying conscious about day-to-day expenses can lead to surprisingly significant improvements in the bigger picture. The great majority of financially successful people have achieved their success as the financial "tortoise" rather than the "hare." A steady plan with consistent follow-through is the time-tested path to True Wealth. Accordingly, we need to keep in mind the overall trajectory of our financial lives. It is important for us to be conscious of our spending habits while at the same attending to proper investing practices. If we attend to conscious spending and proper investing with consistency, we will, over time, build a strong financial structure for our lives.

Choices we make about credit and debt are particularly important in determining our progress toward True Wealth. Consumer debt is, by design, easy to get into and difficult to get out of. The credit card industry is extremely sophisticated and relentless in its marketing. Its focus is on profiting from your debt. Fair enough—there is no injunction against making legal profits from the uninformed consumer. So as a consumer, you have a responsibility to yourself and your family to use credit wisely and to avoid consumer debt. Let's look at how you can use credit wisely—increasing your financial well-being rather than undermining it.

Know Your Credit Score

You, like all consumers, are given a FICO score, a numerical evaluation of overall credit. This score functions more or less like a grade in school, summarizing your credit history. Most creditors base their lending decisions on your FICO score. Scores range from 300 to 850. A variety of factors go into generating your FICO score, including your financial stability, your outstanding balances, and your past payment history. You can go to a variety of internet sites to find your FICO score, including *www.myfico.com* and *www.equifax.com*. The service that we use is called *www.truecredit.com*. For a small annual fee, it provides us a weekly email report on any credit activity and allows us to check our FICO score from time to time.

The higher your FICO score, the less you pay to buy on credit, no matter whether you're getting a home loan, cell phone, a car loan, or signing up for credit cards. As you already know, we encourage you to avoid buying most things on credit. Your home mortgage is of course the great exception, as it is very much in your interest to purchase

> Debt is the slavery of the free.
> ~ Publilius Syrus,
> 1st Century Writer

If your FICO score is	Your interest rate is	Your monthly payment is
760 – 850	6.53%	$1,370.00
700 – 759	6.75%	$1,401.00
680 – 699	6.93%	$1,427.00
660 – 679	7.14%	$1,458.00
640 – 659	7.57%	$1,521.00
620 – 639	8.12%	$1,603.00

your own home with a thirty-year fixed rate mortgage. Based on the rates current on the day that this chapter was written, the following applies to a $216,000 thirty-year, fixed-rate mortgage:

> As you can see in the table to the left, a person with a FICO score of 760 or better will pay $247 less per month than a person with FICO scores below 620— a savings of nearly $2,964 a year. That's a strong incentive to stay on top of your credit situation. The key is avoiding consumer debt as much as possible and making prompt payments on any outstanding balances.

> A good debt is not as good as no debt.
> ~ **Chinese Proverb**

Credit Cards: Nine Steps to Debt Reduction

Credit cards are to the economic body what cigarettes are to the physical body. Although just one probably won't hurt you, using either credit cards or cigarettes over time can be toxic, and they can both be quite addictive. For the rare person who pays them off each month and maintains a zero balance, credit cards can be useful and convenient. For others, however, credit cards can become a serious and debilitating addiction. How serious is this addiction? The average American credit card debt is between $8,500 and $9,000.[1] High interest rates and exorbitant fees make credit cards a bad deal for many Americans and a real hindrance to prosperity.

People who carry credit card debt are not only paying way too much in interest and fees but are also paying dearly for lost opportunity. The misuse of credit cards causes many people to lose opportunities—for their children's education, their professional development, and other life goals. Long-term credit card debt is bad news for anyone seeking the path to True Wealth.

---

1 *Frontline*, "Secret History of the Credit Card," PBS.org, www.pbs.org /wgbh/pages/frontline/shows/credit/etc/synopsis.html.

That said, what if credit cards already have you in their grip? Once you have determined that you want to work on your credit card spending, here are some practical steps you can take:

> Creditors have better memories than debtors.
> ~ **Benjamin Franklin**

- Make a "fearless and searching inventory" of your credit card debt. Face the issue with courage.
- Resolve to stop using credit cards. Replace them with debit cards. If you can't afford something, don't buy it. Save money until you can pay for it in cash.
- List your cards by the interest rates they charge, ranking them from lowest to highest.
- Move your balances to the cards with the lowest rates. Or move balances to a card with a low introductory fee and pay aggressively for those first six months.
- Pledge to yourself to pay off at least 4 percent of the balance each month.
- Pay off your highest interest rate cards first.
- Refinance your home, which will usually give you a more favorable interest rate plus possibly some tax benefits. Refinancing or a home equity loan may be a good alternative to paying off credit card debt. But beware: do not run your credit cards up again.
- Hang in there. Credit cards are seductive and the ensuing debt can be seriously damaging. Do not give up.

I once saw a beautiful woman on the *Today* show who had lost more than two hundred pounds. She explained her success: "I was obese for over thirty years, but I just never gave up. I kept trying until I got there!" So it is with credit card debt. Never give up. Keep trying until you get that monkey off your back. With your credit card debt eliminated, you will have taken a giant step on the path toward True Wealth. You can do it!

Cars, Auto Loans, and Auto Insurance

Second only to a house, the automobile is the most valuable asset most Americans own. If you're in the market for a car, here are some helpful hints for using your money to best effect.

First, give some thought to how important your car is to your self-image. If you are in a high-profile business (a real estate broker, for instance), investing in a new, high-end car will be a necessary investment. Maybe you're simply someone who enjoys and takes a lot of pride in the car you drive. In that case, you may want to allocate some of your "recreation" budget toward buying and maintaining an expensive car. The important point here is not to choose a particular kind of car—new, used, luxury, or budget—but rather to choose with awareness. If you see your car simply as a means of getting from here to there, don't let yourself be seduced by ubiquitous commercials into spending more than is necessary.

Financially, you are almost always better off buying a late-model, quality used car than a new one. *Consumer Reports* once published research showing that a reliable used car offers the most for your money. That's not particularly surprising news. However, what *was* surprising was that even an unreliable used car, requiring numerous repairs, offered better value than a new car!

You can save thousands by buying used, and you can usually do better buying from a private party than from a dealership or used car lot. A good resource for used cars is the *Consumer Reports* website, *www.consumerreports.org*, which ranks used cars. Buy a car ranked high for safety and low for rate of repairs. Our last car purchase was a four-year-old Honda Accord. Our other car is a Lexus that we also bought used. These cars had the safety and reliability rankings we were looking for. It is also ideal if you are able to save enough to buy a used car with cash. If you need to finance your car, though, make sure to shop around for your best loan. We

> Credit buying is much like being drunk. The buzz happens immediately and gives you a lift. ... The hangover comes the day after.
> ~ **Dr. Joyce Brothers, Psychologist**

recommend *www.bankrate.com* for its excellent tools and resources for shopping a car loan. You might be surprised at the amount you can save by taking a little extra time to shop for a loan.

If you choose to purchase a new car, then you will be faced with the decision of whether to lease or to buy. Here is the short answer: it is almost always better to buy. When you buy a car with a loan, you are building *equity* in the car. If you keep the car, you will eventually own it free and clear. However, leasing a car is like renting your home rather than buying it. The dealer or leasing agency will take possession of the car after your contract is up. The lure is low up-front costs and the opportunity to drive an upscale car for a seemingly lower cost. Before you sign on the dotted line of a lease agreement, consider the following words of caution:

> Another way to solve the traffic problems of this country is to pass a law that only paid-for cars be allowed to use the highways.
> ~ **Will Rogers, Humorist**

- Leases are written by lawyers who work for the car dealer. The fine print will favor the dealer in ways that are not immediately apparent.
- A lease does not give you ownership or equity in the car.
- Dealers charge heavy fees on early returns, so getting out of a lease prior to its termination date will be costly.
- Dealers charge fees if you put on more than the specified number of miles.
- Dealers charge hefty fees for any cosmetic or mechanical damage.

The long and short of it is that buying a late-model used car with an excellent repair and safety record is the best way to go. Make sure to have a qualified mechanic check it out before you buy it.

It is smart to shop for auto insurance, too, and the internet is a fantastic medium for getting a good price.

Visit the auto section of *www.insure.com*, which will generate quote comparisons for you.

Liability coverage is the most important part of your auto insurance coverage—don't skimp on that part of the policy. The additional cost of higher limits is usually not that great and is worth the price if you can afford it. Liability coverage is expressed as a series of three limits, for instance $100,000/$300,000/$50,000, which means:

- The maximum amount the insurance company will pay for bodily injuries to any one person in an accident is $100,000.
- The maximum amount the insurance company will pay for all bodily injuries for all people hurt in an accident is $300,000.
- The maximum amount the insurance company will pay for damages to another person's property in an accident is $50,000.

> A man in debt is so far a slave.
> ~ **Ralph Waldo Emerson**

We recommend that you go well above these minimums. Auto liability coverage is usually available with limits up to $1 million. Go for maximum coverage, but shop around for the best price.

In Summary

In this chapter, we have shown the smart way of dealing with debt, credit cards, and automobile purchasing. Remember:

- Take care of the dollars, and the thousands of dollars will take care of themselves.
- Be the financial tortoise rather than the hare, and you'll win the race.
- Check your FICO score yearly at least.
- Pay off your credit cards in full each month. Keep your balances at zero.

- Build equity in your car by buying instead of leasing.
- Buy a late-model used car rather than a new car.
- Get good coverage for auto insurance, but shop around for the best price.

He looks the whole world in the face for he owes not any man.

~ Henry Wadsworth
   Longfellow, Poet

ADEQUATE INSURANCE:
Caring for Yourself and Your Family

16

<u>Six Pillars of True Wealth</u>
Smart Investing
Home Ownership
Empowered Earning
Conscious Spending and Credit
Adequate Insurance
Wise Planning

> I am prepared for the worst but hope for the best.
> ~ Benjamin Disraeli, Former British Prime Minister

It is all too easy to be lulled into the belief that "it won't happen to me." No one likes to think about the possibility of disaster, and considering questions of insurance can be uncomfortable and anxiety-provoking. However, this is an area where you must call on your higher wisdom and remember the admonition "Trust in God but tie your camel."

Owning sufficient insurance plays a vital role in your economic well-being. It allows you to protect yourself against the financial risk of devastating loss by transferring that risk to an insurance company.

In this chapter, you will learn what kinds of insurance you need, given your stage in life and your commitments and responsibilities. We will explore:

- Health insurance
- Life insurance
- Long-term care insurance
- Disability insurance

Health Insurance

Health insurance is a must for any American. A health crisis can be truly devastating to your financial well-being. Many Americans are provided with health insurance through their place of employment. If this is not true for you, or if you prefer alternative medical approaches not covered by most insurance plans, you may want to consider one of the new cost-effective Health Savings Account plans (HSA plans), which consist of high deductible health insurance along with a health savings account. HSA plans replaced Medical Savings Accounts (MSA plans) in federal legislation signed in December 2003. They represent a considerable improvement over MSA plans.

Here is how HSA plans work: first, you purchase a high deductible health insurance plan. You are then qualified to open a Health Savings Account, which is a tax-sheltered savings account similar to an IRA. Unlike an IRA, which is for retirement savings, the purpose of an HSA is to save for healthcare expenses. Deposits are tax-deferred and can be withdrawn tax-free and penalty-free by check or debit card to pay for qualified healthcare expenses, such as over-the-counter and prescription medicines, with pre-tax dollars. If you have high medical costs in a given year, your health insurance kicks in once your deductible is met. Premiums on high-deductible health insurance are generally much less expensive than premiums on health insurance with low deductibles.

HSA funds can be used to pay for expenses associated with the diagnosis, cure, treatment, or prevention of illness or injury. This includes doctor's office visits, medications (both over-the-counter and prescription), dental expenses (including orthodontia), vision expenses, psychotherapy, acupuncture, and chiropractic. Cosmetic surgery usually

> I got the bill for my surgery. Now I know what those doctors were wearing masks for.
> ~ James H. Boren,
> American Public Servant

does not qualify under the plan, but laser eye surgery does. Another interesting feature is that you can use HSA funds to pay long-term care insurance premiums.[1]

If you have money left in your HSA at the end of the year, those funds stay in the account and continue to earn interest on a tax-favored basis. These funds can be used to pay for future medical expenses or can be saved for retirement. If there are funds in the account when you reach age sixty-five, those funds can be used for retirement expenses in much the same way IRA funds are used in retirement.[2]

How much can be contributed to an HSA? The IRS issues official maximum contribution levels. In 2006 for taxpayers with self-only coverage, the maximum contribution was $2,700; for family coverage, the maximum was $5,450. For every month that a qualified health plan is active, one-twelfth of the maximum annual allowable contribution can be deposited into an HSA.

A good source of information on HSAs is the U.S. Department of Treasury website, *www.treas.gov*. Enter HSA in the search box, and it will bring up a list of articles with valuable and up-to-date information. Major health insurers such as Blue Shield, Aetna, and Blue Cross have useful information as well.

An HSA plan along with a high-deductible health insurance policy could save you money both on taxes and on your healthcare expenses. With today's high health care costs, an HSA plan is an option you may want to explore.

Life Insurance: Do You Need It?

Life insurance is the most unselfish of investments. It provides for those who will survive you. If someone is dependent on you

> Precaution is better than cure.
> ~ Edward Coke, Jurist

---

1 Consult with a qualified tax accountant to make certain that your medical expenses qualify for Health Savings Account tax-free treatment.

2 Distributions for nonqualified expenses are considered taxable income and are subject to a 10 percent penalty.

for income and you wish to continue to provide for that person after your death, then you almost certainly need life insurance. The classic scenario illustrating the need for life insurance is the young family in which the children will need continued support in the event of the death of one or both parents. Another classic scenario is a couple where one spouse is the breadwinner. It is frequently wise to insure the life of the income-earning spouse so that the surviving spouse will be taken care of.

From our financial planning practice, we learned of Sheila, whose father died when she was six. She was one of four children. He left the family destitute. He had no life insurance. Sheila's mother struggled mightily to keep the children fed and sheltered, and Sheila still carries a sense of loss, sadness, and bitterness that her father "didn't care enough about us to go ahead and buy life insurance."

How Much Do You Need?

There are a variety of ways to calculate your life insurance needs. Feedback from your financial planner may in fact be the best way for you to arrive at a figure, as he or she should know your financial situation in detail. However, here is one approach that can be useful:

1. Determine your family income.
2. Multiply that number by 0.8.
3. Divide that number by a reasonable rate of return on your life insurance proceeds (many planners assume an 8 percent return on investment, although we prefer the more conservative figure of 6 percent).
4. Subtract savings and investments you currently own.

The above steps will provide you with an estimated amount of insurance needed to replace current income. If there will be increasing expenses such as higher education for the kids or care for an elderly parent, then you will need to take that into account.

> The lives and happiness of our children as far ahead as the mind can reach, depend on us today.
> ~ Carl A. Berendsen,
>   New Zealand Diplomat

Consider the case of Jason and Marcia. Jason makes $100,000 at his sales job and Marcia makes $50,000 at her administrative job with the post office. They have two children: Susan, an eighth grader, and Lawrence, a third grader. Jason and Marcia have $125,000 in investments and savings. Let's see how much life insurance they might need.

1. Combine their income and multiply it by 0.8. Jason and Marsha's combined income is $150,000. We discount this number by 20 percent since the family will no longer need to support Jason after his death: $150,000 × 0.8 = $120,000.

2. Since Marcia may need to work only part-time in order to take full responsibility for the children, let's assume her continuing income will be $35,000. We will subtract her ongoing income from the income we need to replace with insurance: $120,000 − 35,000 = $85,000.

3. Now we need to divide this figure by a reasonable rate of return on the investments they make with the insurance proceeds. We go with a conservative estimate of 6 percent. This gives us the amount of principal needed to generate income sufficient to meet the survivor's income needs: $85,000 ÷ 0.06 = $1,416,666.

4. We reduce this figure by the amount they have in savings, $125,000: $1,416,666 − $125,000 = $1,291,666.

> I detest life insurance agents: they always argue that I shall some day die, which is not so.
> ~ **Stephen B. Leacock,**
> **19th Century Canadian**
> **Politician, Writer**

We now have a ballpark figure for the amount of life insurance Marcia will need on Jason's life: $1,291,666.

Let's turn to Jason's needs in the event of Marcia's death.

1. Take the combined income and reduce by 20 percent, as the income needed to support Marcia is no

longer necessary in the event of her death: $150,000 × 0.8 = $120,000.

2. Jason will continue to work, but is less available to earn a full-time income due to increased parental responsibilities. We figure his continuing income at $80,000 and subtract that figure from the figure above: $120,000 − $80,000 = $40,000.

3. We divide the above figure by our 6 percent presumed rate of return: $40,000 ÷ 0.06 = $666,666.

4. We subtract their current investments from the above figure: $666,666 − $125,000 = $541,666.

We now have a ballpark idea of the amount of insurance Jason needs to insure Marcia's life: $541,666.

> Chance favors the prepared mind.
> ~ **Louis Pasteur, French Biologist and Chemist**

Again, we recommend that you work with your financial planner on an analysis of your life insurance needs, but if you apply the above method to your circumstances, you should have a pretty good idea of how much life insurance would be right for you. For further help in calculating your life insurance needs, go to our website, *www.insightfinancialgroup.com*, and follow the links to calculators, and then to insurance calculators.

What Kind of Life Insurance Is Right for You?

There are two basic types of life insurance: temporary and permanent. Temporary, or term insurance, does not build up a cash value and simply provides a death benefit for a given period of time. Permanent insurance, on the other hand, is designed to last until the death of the insured and does build up a cash value. Varieties of permanent insurance include whole life insurance, universal life insurance, and variable universal life insurance. For the present discussion, let us focus first on whether term insurance or permanent insurance is right for you. Next, we will go on to consider the question of which type of term or permanent insurance you may find most advantageous.

The rule of thumb for term insurance is this: if your need is temporary, then temporary life insurance should do the trick. A case where this might apply would be a family with two working parents and young kids. Should one or both parents die, the children will need additional support. However, unless the parents feel it is necessary to support the children after they reach adulthood, that need will decrease when the children finish college, say at age twenty-three. If the youngest child were thirteen, then perhaps a ten-year term policy would be sufficient to meet the temporary need of supporting the children. Term insurance is far less costly than permanent insurance.

The rule of thumb for permanent insurance is a permanent need for insurance. A case where this might apply would be a situation where there is an ongoing need for income for the surviving partner. This kind of situation is common for self-employed people and people who are not part of a traditional pension plan that pays lifetime benefits. For example, take Lisa and Judith, who are domestic partners. Lisa is a physical therapist in private practice, and Judith is a public school teacher. They have no children. Although Judith has a pension through her school district, the district does not allow same-sex domestic partners to be included in joint and survivor benefits. If Lisa predeceases Judith, then Judith will be OK because of her pension. On the other hand, if Judith predeceases Lisa, then Lisa will have an ongoing need for retirement income. Permanent insurance can meet that need.

People with high net worth frequently choose permanent insurance also. David and Katie are one couple who have done this. David is an attorney making more than $500,000 per year. Katie is a pediatrician making more than $200,000 per year. They have extensive securities investments and real estate holdings and expect to inherit

> There is no value in life except what you choose to place upon it and no happiness in any place except what you bring it yourself.
> ~ **Henry David Thoreau**

several million more when Katie's father dies. Their need for insurance is driven by the fact they will owe extensive estate taxes and do not want their children to be in a position of needing to come up with a large amount of tax money when David and Katie die. If the estate tax is eventually repealed, then they are happy to have the insurance money to add to their children's inheritance. The purpose of the permanent life insurance is to cover any estate taxes that will be due.

If you determine that permanent life insurance is right for you, then you will need to decide which kind fits you best.

Whole life insurance

Whole life insurance provides you with a fixed rate of return on the savings portion of your insurance and has a fixed premium. Ordinary whole life insurance gives you a fixed payment amount on the assumption that you will pay the premiums for the rest of your life. As you pay into the policy over the years, you may have options other than retaining the policy until you die. For example, you may be able to use dividends to pay the policy off in a shorter amount of time, surrender the policy in favor of an annuity, or trade the policy in for a smaller amount of paid-up insurance. Whole life insurance provides permanent insurance for the lowest premium dollar and has limited but important flexibility as your life circumstances change.

Universal life insurance

Another approach to permanent life insurance is universal life insurance, which offers flexible premiums and allows the policy owner to take money out of the account without taking a loan. With universal life, you do not direct the investments in your cash value. Instead, the insurance company gives you a fixed rate of return. With universal life, you can choose a level death benefit or an increasing death

> Family is the most important thing in the world.
> ~ **Princess Diana**

benefit. This insurance offers flexible premiums and allows you to take money out of the account through loans or partial withdrawals. Any withdrawals or loans will reduce your cash value and/or death benefit. The level death benefit maintains the same death benefit while the amount owned in the cash value increases. Your other choice is an increasing death benefit. Under this scenario, the death benefit rises as the amount you own in the cash value rises. If you are looking for more flexibility than a whole life policy offers but want a fixed rate of return on your cash value, then universal life insurance may work well for you.

> By failing to prepare, you are preparing to fail.
> ~ Benjamin Franklin

Variable universal life insurance

Both of us own variable universal life insurance (VUL), since it fits our particular circumstances. This insurance provides permanent insurance along with cash value like whole life or universal life. A unique feature of VUL is that you direct investments in the cash balance, with stock and bond investments in separate accounts that pool the resources of many investors and are professionally managed. The money management firms that run many of these separate accounts are leading investment companies, well-respected in the field. Most VUL policies offer a fairly wide range of investment choices, typically with a variety of familiar money management firms. There are even VULs that have a variety of socially responsible investment choices available in the subaccounts. If you are looking for maximum flexibility in permanent insurance, a VUL policy may be an investment to consider.

Permanent Insurance Is for the Long Haul

With any permanent insurance, it is important that you make a serious commitment to staying with the policy over the long haul. Canceling these policies after just a few years can be quite costly. If you close out the policy in the early years, the insurer will likely impose surrender charges that reduce the cash value of the policy. If permanent insurance helps you meet your financial planning and/or estate planning goals, and you plan on sticking with it over the long haul, then permanent insurance may play a vital role in your financial life. If, on the other hand, you have only a time-limited need for life insurance, then relatively inexpensive term insurance is probably right for you.

Long-Term Care Insurance

In 2006 the average cost of long-term care in the United States was $70,000 per year. The California Department of Health Services reports, "More than 40 percent of those who turn sixty-five will spend some time in a nursing home." Of those who enter nursing homes, "55 percent will have a lifetime use of at least one year, 24 percent will stay between one and five years, and 21 percent will have a total lifetime use of five years or more."[3]

Clearly, the danger of a devastatingly expensive stay in a long-term care facility is a real one. Long-term care insurance (LTC) can be sensible and even extremely important for many people, but it is not for everyone. People who will benefit most from LTC are those with a range of assets between $150,000 and $1.5 million. A little background will explain why people within this middle range of assets are best suited to LTC.

You cannot rely on Medicare for your long-term care coverage. Medicaid currently pays for long-term care but only if you have extremely limited assets. Think of LTC as insurance for your assets, so that you do not have to spend your assets down in order to qualify for Medicaid to pay for your long-term care bed.

LTC may not be necessary if you have a high net worth, but if your assets are less than $1.5 million and

> Have the courage to face a difficulty lest it kick you harder than you bargained for.
> ~ Stanislaus I,
>   18th Century
>   King of Poland

---

3 *California Partnership for Long Term Care: Consumer Information*. www.dhs.cahwnet
.gov/cpltc/html/consumer.htm

more than $150,000 you might want to consider this kind of insurance. If your assets are high enough, then you probably will not need the coverage because you could pay for care out-of-pocket and still protect sufficient assets for your heirs. If your net worth is low enough, then you may be able to spend down your assets until Medicaid can kick in.

Here are some long-term care guidelines. The younger you are and the better your health, the lower your premiums will be. On the other hand, these same favorable health conditions mean that you may be paying into your policy for many years and never need it.

We often counsel our clients to purchase LTC in their mid-fifties. Another issue is home care and assisted living care. Make sure that, if you want these options, they are written into your policy. Some policies cover only skilled nursing facilities, which would be less desirable than assisted living or home care for many consumers.

One way to save money on your policy is to increase your elimination period—the waiting period before your benefits kick in. Do not save money on your policy by eliminating the inflation coverage. We recommend to all of our clients that they choose a 5 percent compound inflation coverage so that spiraling healthcare costs do not overtake the coverage in the LTC policy. Make a few calls to the better LTC facilities in the area to check on their costs. Then design your policy around what you will need. With the 5 percent compound inflation rider, today's coverage should keep pace with inflation. One client of mine knows that if she were ever to need care, she would want to be at the finest facility in New York City—the same facility her mother was in for seven years. We called their intake worker to check on costs: the facility charges a whopping $400 per day, or $146,000 per year. As you can imagine, we designed a very high-end policy for her. Still, if you figure an average facility cost of $191 per day, you can find sensi-

> Old age ain't no place for sissies.
> ~ H. L. Mencken, Journalist

ble coverage at a reasonable price, if you do your research. As with all insurance, you must look for the balance between the premium you are willing to pay and the coverage you want.

Look for an insurer with solid financial ratings and one that has been in the long-term care insurance business for at least ten years. Some newcomers to the field may charge low premiums in the beginning, but you are more likely to deal with insolvency or premium hikes if you do not choose an established player in the field. A source of independent insurance ratings is available through Standard and Poors, *www.standardandpoors.com*, which will give you financial solvency information that is important in choosing an insurer. You obviously want your insurer to be around and able to pay claims if the need arises, so do your research. Your financial advisor should also be able to help you find the right company and design an appropriate policy.

Disability Insurance

If you are self-employed or if your employer does not provide it, then you should consider disability insurance coverage. If your extended family has money that can be available to you in an emergency, if you have significant investments that generate income, or if your spouse or domestic partner can support your household, then replacing your income in the event of disability becomes less urgent. If you are dependent on the income you earn, however, disability insurance can be an important investment to make.

A number of our clients have been confused about the difference between disability insurance and long-term care insurance, so let us take a moment to differentiate them. Long-term care insurance covers the cost of your care if you become unable to manage the activities of daily living on your own. For example, a person with Alzheimer's may live for many years but be unable to take care of himself or her-

> You know the value of every merchandize, yet you do not know your own value.
>
> ~ Rumi

self. Disability insurance provides income replacement for people who had been working but are currently unable to work due to an injury or illness. An example of this need is the self-employed person who has an accident and cannot return to work for a number of years while she is recovering.

Disability insurance policies vary widely in their quality. Unfortunately, high-quality policies are expensive: expect to pay I to 3 percent of your annual income. Here are some things to look for in a disability policy.

Definition of disability

Some policies use a definition of disability as restrictive as that used by Social Security (i.e. the insured cannot work at any occupation). This restrictive definition is problematic for anyone who cares about returning to his or her own profession after a disability. Say a teacher had a stroke and needed speech rehabilitation before she could function again in her classroom, despite being able to do some other kind of work. She would want disability insurance that defines disability as the inability to function in one's "own occupation" so that she could receive benefits until she is ready to return to the classroom.

Partial disability benefits

We have a client who works as a chef and suffered a serious stroke. Following six months of total disability, he now works part-time. Partial disability benefits continue to cover him to help him make up the difference between his old full-time income and the income he can now generate on a part-time basis. Partial or residual disability benefits are designed to make up the difference between income prior to disability and income earned during disability. Also, if your income tends to fluctuate, look for a policy that defines prior income to be the greater of two base periods so that you are not penalized by defining your income during a slump in your earnings.

> Nothing can bring you peace but yourself.
> ~ Ralph Waldo Emerson

Noncancelable and guaranteed renewable

You do not want a policy that will be canceled if you begin to develop a medical problem, so you should look for a policy that is either noncancelable or guaranteed renewable. A noncancelable policy is best, as it locks in rates and benefits. Guaranteed renewable means that your policy can't be canceled, but the insurer reserves the right to raise premiums for specific reasons. Least desirable is a conditionally renewable contract. An insurer can raise premiums at any time on these policies. Avoid policies that can raise your premium on an individual rather than a class basis. Some companies will offer guaranteed renewability to age sixty-five and then conditional renewability to age seventy-five.

Elimination period

Disability policies have an elimination period, or waiting period, before benefits become available. Of course, you can save on premiums with a longer elimination period; typical options are thirty, sixty, ninety, and 120 days. If you have savings or other sources of short-term income, you can save premium dollars by opting for a longer elimination period.

Duration of disability

How long your policy pays for disability is of course a key provision. Obviously the longer your benefit duration, the higher your premium will be. Duration periods can be as little as two years or as long as until the insured reaches age sixty-five, when Social Security kicks in. Some carriers even offer a lifetime duration period. The choices you make regarding this provision of your policy can have a lasting impact on the financial health of you and your family, so think carefully about this provision in the context of your overall financial situation.

Cost of living adjustments

Many insurers offer cost of living adjustments as an option and also allow you to decide the percentage rate used to calculate the adjustment. As with other features in your disability policy, a higher level of benefit will normally equal a higher premium. Younger people in particular are well-advised to add an inflation rider to their coverage to insure that their benefit amount will keep pace with inflation.

Taxation Issues

For a self-employed person who pays taxes as a sole-proprietor, disability insurance premiums do not qualify as a tax deduction. The good news, however, is that the benefits are nontaxable. Disability insurance provided by an employer is a tax deduction for the employer, but the benefits are taxable to the beneficiary. Let's say that an administrator is employed at a nonprofit agency three-quarters time and does about eight hours a week of consulting to other agencies as a side business. She has disability insurance through the nonprofit agency, which provides 60 percent replacement coverage of her agency income. Should she become disabled, that disability income will be subject to income taxes, significantly reducing her replacement income. It may be prudent for her to consider supplementing her agency policy with one she purchases herself.

> In this world nothing is certain but death and taxes.
> ~ **Benjamin Franklin**

The Courage to Face the Possibility of Disability

It is an act of courage to face the fact that disability can happen to you. It is all too easy to live in denial about the possibility and consequences of a disability. However, if you purchase a quality insurance policy and end up needing it, you will thank yourself many times over for having made the investment.

Exercise: Check-in with Your Feelings

As we said at the beginning of this chapter, insurance is not a pleasant subject to contemplate. It's likely that any number of negative feelings have come up as you read through this chapter. Perhaps your Superego is telling you, "You should have taken care of all this long ago. When are you going to grow up?" Or you may be thinking, "This is more than I can deal with. I need someone to take care of these things for me."

By this point in the book, you know that bringing feelings to awareness and accepting that "feelings are neither wrong nor right, they just are" is the first step toward integrating your feelings and taking action.

Start a page in your Money Journal to jot down the feelings that arise as you think about insurance in all its permutations. Do your best to be gentle with yourself. Breathe as you experience the feelings and notice any physical manifestations. Don't make an effort to change anything about the way you're feeling. Remind yourself that you don't have to make any decisions today.

Remind yourself that it's important to ask for help when you need it. Remind yourself that you don't need to be an expert. Remind yourself of all the steps you have already taken on the road to developing your True Self. See if you can look at making decisions about insurance as an opportunity to expand your consciousness in a new direction. Rather than contracting in anxiety, allow yourself to open in curiosity.

> Take time to repair the roof when the sun is shining.
> ~ John F. Kennedy

WISE PLANNING:
Essentials of Estate Planning

17

Six Pillars of True Wealth
Smart Investing
Home Ownership
Empowered Earning
Conscious Spending and Credit
Adequate Insurance
Wise Planning

> Life is not separate from death.
> It only looks that way.
> **~ Blackfoot Proverb**

"**To suffer one's own death** and be reborn is not easy." So said Fritz Perls, the father of Gestalt therapy. To work with the issues involved in estate planning we must be willing to acknowledge our own mortality and that of our loved ones. This can be emotionally challenging but also very rewarding. Recognizing the impermanence of life can lead to a new appreciation of life's preciousness. Dealing responsibly with end-of-life concerns offers peace of mind and a sense of providing comfort and protection to those who will survive us.

Certainly, no matter what your net worth, you owe it to yourself and your family to think about how money will be dealt with after you or your spouse passes away. Estate planning also includes instructions regarding your medical preferences should you become unable to express them.

Leaving behind a well-considered estate plan provides for survivors, and helps to leave a legacy of love.

Estate planning is not a project to undertake on your own. We strongly recommend that you consult with a qualified financial planner and an estate-planning attorney to design and implement your plan. Our purpose in writing this chapter is simply to orient you to the issues involved in estate planning and to introduce you to effective strategies.

The first step in creating your estate plan is to determine your goals. After these are established, your financial planner and an estate-planning attorney can work with you as a team to implement them. Below are some estate-planning goals for you to consider:

> *Organizing is what you do before you do something, so that when you do it, it is not all mixed up.*
>
> **~ A. A. Milne, Writer**

- Put advanced medical directives in place.
- Appoint a financial power of attorney.
- Create a living trust.
- Create a pour-over will.
- Minimize the probate process.
- Make provisions for the guardianship of your minor children.
- Establish Planned Charitable Giving.
- Minimize estate and income taxes.
- Assure that your home will be available to your partner while he or she lives, then pass to your children.
- Assure that your estate is divided fairly among your heirs.
- Protect your own financial security in the event that your partner dies before you.

The five most important documents in your estate plan are:

1. Durable power of attorney for healthcare
2. Living will
3. Financial power of attorney

4. Living trust
5. Pour-over will

Put Advanced Medical Directives in Place (Durable Power of Attorney for Healthcare and Living Will)

Many years ago, I (Peter) worked at the University of California Davis Medical Center as a social worker in the hospice program. Here is just one story out of many that underline the importance of setting up advanced medical directives. The patient was a forty-year-old man with Lou Gehrig's disease (ALS). He was gradually losing motor control, but he was quite intact cognitively. I discussed on several occasions the importance of clarifying his wishes, should he need to be put on life support. He told his family and me that he did not want extraordinary measures taken if there was no chance of recovery, but he avoided putting his wishes into a legal document. Sadly, he was rushed, semi-conscious, to the hospital where he was eventually put on life support even though his treating physicians all agreed that there was no chance of recovery. His family did not want him to suffer further and even his minister asked that no heroic medical measures be taken. He died two months later, but his family was hit hard by the medical bills and by the emotional toll of this unnecessary prolongation of his suffering.

> Regardless of your stance on the right-to-die issue or the seven-year legal battle waging over [Terri] Schiavo, this case emphasizes the importance of completing advance medical directives—living wills and powers of attorney. Schiavo never completed any advance medical directives. If she had, the fighting and bitterness felt on both sides may have been avoided.
> **~ State Bar of Texas**

Advanced medical directives are your chance to give instruction about the level of treatment you want in case you are rendered unconscious or incompetent. Say you were in a car crash and were brought to the emergency room brain-dead and with no chance of recovery. Would you want to be kept alive indefinitely on life support machines without regard to the cost to your family? Would you want to appoint someone to act as your agent? These are the questions to be addressed in your advanced medical directives so that your family can have the peace of mind and legal standing they will need to carry out your wishes.

You can use a medical power of attorney to assure that your wishes are carried out. To do this, you designate a person whom you trust to carry out your wishes. The person you choose is known as your "agent." An estate-planning attorney can draw up these papers for you. You are free to revoke this at any time, and you can make more than one person your agent. If you sit down with the person you want to appoint and discuss your values and wishes with them, they will feel much more comfortable about carrying out difficult decisions on your behalf.

Create a Living Will

A living will spells out what specific medical treatments you do and do not want in the event that you have been rendered incapable of making medical decisions. In your living will you specify such things as whether or not you want to be resuscitated, or whether or not you wish to be put on artificial respiration.

Though it is not easy to make plans for an eventuality you hope will never happen, it is through the awareness of your own mortality that you become most fully engaged in life. Buddhism teaches us that the only constant is change and that life is by its very nature impermanent. Working with end-of-life issues helps you to hold the consciousness of impermanence while at the same time fully invest in this life by taking responsibility for yourself and your family. Keep this knowledge in mind if you are feeling anxious about end-of-life issues.

Appoint a Financial Power of Attorney

A financial power of attorney is similar to a medical power of attorney. In both, you name an agent to carry out your wishes—in this case your financial wishes—should you be rendered unable to do so for yourself due to illness or injury. Having an agent in place can be a great benefit to your family, saving them the ordeal of having a court grant

A durable power of attorney for finances—or financial power of attorney—is a simple, inexpensive, and reliable way to arrange for someone to manage your finances if you become unable to do so yourself.

~ Shae Irving, J.D.

this power. You can give your agent as much or as little power over your finances as you wish. Commonly, people give the agent authority to handle:

- Paying bills
- Collecting social security and other benefits
- Banking and financial transactions
- Maintaining property
- Investing and managing retirement accounts

Your agent is obligated to act in your best interests and must not act with conflict of interest. You can revoke the financial power of attorney at any time, and it will only come into play should you become incapacitated. The financial power of attorney ends at your death—after that point it is no longer in effect. If you create a living trust as we discuss below, you may want to appoint the same person to be the trustee of the living trust and or executor of your pour-over will in the event of your incompetence or death.

> A man who does not think and plan long ahead will find trouble right at his door.
> ~ **Confucius**

Create a Living Trust and Minimize Probate

When Elvis Presley died, his estate was worth more than $10 million. After his estate went through the probate process, its value was diminished to $3 million. Over 70 percent of his estate went to pay appraisal costs, legal fees, executor's fees, and estate taxes. Probate is the process of proving a will's validity in court and executing the provisions of the will under the guidance of the court. As was the case with Elvis's estate, probate can be costly and time-consuming. Even uncomplicated estates can take six months or more to sort through. A living trust allows you to bypass the probate process, as the property in the trust passes by operation of law directly to your beneficiaries.

Creating a living trust can be an effective method for you to efficiently pass on many assets according to your wishes. You can create your living trust to be revocable, meaning that you can rescind, amend, or terminate it at any time. A typical arrangement is that you create the trust and appoint yourself to be the holder of the property, or the trustee. Once you have created the trust, you change the title of the property from your own name to the name of the trust. Within the trust, you appoint another trustee who will take over in the event of your death or incompetence. Your living trust does not change the tax picture for you or for your estate, but it can help accomplish other important goals, such as avoiding probate and passing on your assets after your death according to your wishes.

Here are the major advantages of creating a living trust:

- Property passes from you to your beneficiaries without the need for probate.
- If you own property in more than one state, you can avoid repeating probate by putting the property in your living trust in the state where you reside. You avoid ancillary jurisdiction of out-of-state property by titling it in your living trust.
- When property goes through probate, the records are made public. With a living trust, you avoid probate and the public record of private financial information.
- A living trust is relatively easy to set up and change. (There are useful self-help books—notably from Nolo Press—but we strongly recommend that you use an attorney.)
- Living trusts are difficult to contest, whereas, in general, wills are more vulnerable.
- Living trusts may help you to consolidate your assets and organize better. As you add property to the trust, you must think about its disposition and management.

The types of property that are commonly transferred into the living trust include:

> Four steps to achievement: Plan purposefully. Prepare prayerfully. Proceed positively. Pursue persistently.
> ~ **William A. Ward, Writer**

- Real estate
- Bank accounts
- Brokerage accounts
- Stock and bond certificates
- Vehicles and boats

Retitling your property in the name of your trust is usually a pretty simple procedure. Let's say that Jane Smith has just created, with the help of an attorney, "The Jane Smith Revocable Living Trust, Dated July 15, 2006." She owns a car in her own name. She fills out the motor vehicle department paperwork to change ownership from "Jane Smith" to "The Jane Smith Revocable Living Trust, Dated July 15, 2006." She changes the titles to her home, brokerage account, and bank account as well. Now her living trust owns those assets. As trustee of the living trust, Jane retains full control over these assets, can use them for whatever purposes she chooses, and is responsible for taxes and upkeep as before. The difference lies in the disposition of those assets after her death.

> If you have a living trust, then your will is often referred to as a *pour-over* will. That will provides that any assets held in your name at your death and not in your living trust will be added to the trust to be held, administered, and distributed according to the terms of the trust.
> **~ California State Bar**

Create a Pour-over Will

The revocable living trust allows you to detail the disposition of property that is titled in the name of the trust. Your property that is not specifically owned by the trust is not included in the trust. So, you will need a will to direct property not already owned by your living trust to either be bequeathed to the trust or to individuals. This is where the "pour-over" will comes into play. You appoint an executor of your pour-over will; this could be the same person who is the agent in your financial power of attorney and trustee of your living trust. You instruct that the assets not titled in your trust be poured into the trust at your death.

It is virtually impossible to title everything you own in the name of your living trust. Much property such as jewelry, clothes, your favorite vase, that special book of poetry, the family Bible, and so on are quite difficult to title at all. You may detail in the pour-over will who gets whatever is not titled in the name of the trust. All items that are not otherwise named in the pour-over will or titled in the name of the trust can be directed to pour into the trust, to be divided among your heirs according to its provisions. In your pour-over will you may also address your wishes as to funeral and burial arrangements.

Make Provisions for Your Minor Children

Probably the most important issue in any will is the appointment of guardianship for your minor children. This issue can be addressed in your pour-over will. We suggest that you discuss the matter of guardianship with the future guardian, and have a frank discussion about the emotional and financial issues involved. It is easy to dismiss the possibility that death or incompetence may take you away from your children, but we know that such scenarios are being played out each and every day. It is best to prepare for these unforeseen circumstances so that your children are provided for. If the best people to care for the children will need financial help to do so, then life insurance held in trust for the benefit of the children may be necessary as a way to finance their future needs.

Establish Planned Charitable Giving

In chapter 2 we discussed the spiritual dimension of charitable giving. Charitable giving can also be a key part of your estate-planning process. You can give to your favorite charity in your estate plan with a number of well-established techniques for planned giving. While we won't go into the details of the many different avenues here, be aware that there are commonly used strategies that you can explore. Consult an estate-planning attorney, as the field of planned giving can get rather complex and should be integrated into your overall estate plan.

> Let us put our minds together and see what life we can make for our children.
> ~ Sitting Bull

Minimize Estate and Income Taxes

Many people mistakenly assume that estate taxes will not apply to them because they think that estate taxes apply only to the wealthy. They may not be adding up their assets in the same way the IRS does. When the IRS figures the value of your estate they take into account your home, investments, personal property, retirement accounts, and all insurance that you own. You might be surprised what these combined values add up to. While estate taxes are a major political foot-ball these days, here are the amounts beyond which estate taxes will be owed, according to the law as it now stands:

Year	Amount Excluded from Estate Taxation
2006	$2,000,000
2007	$2,000,000
2008	$2,000,000
2009	$3,500,000
2010	Unlimited
2011	$1,000,000

> Taxes, after all, are dues that we pay for the privileges of membership in an organized society.
> ~ **Franklin D. Roosevelt**

The above table shows the amount that your estate can exclude from taxation. If these changing amounts are confusing, it's because the whole issue is very political. We think it's unlikely that estate taxes will be eliminated for two reasons:

1. We believe that budget deficits will compel Congress to keep the estate tax in place.
2. We believe that the mandates of good public policy will prevail, and we feel that maintaining the estate tax remains a wise public policy.

Despite our opinion that the estate tax is a fair and sensible form of taxation when designed properly, we are committed to helping our clients keep their estate tax liabilities to a minimum. In the year 2011 and beyond, estate taxes are due on estates valued at $1 million or more. Here are some well-accepted strategies for minimizing estate taxes.

Credit Shelter Trusts

Let's assume that you are planning for the year 2011 or beyond and the exclusion amount on the estate tax is $1 million, meaning that estate taxes are due on amounts above $1 million in your estate. Because you can leave your spouse an unlimited amount of money with no estate tax, many people pass all of their assets to their spouse. However, a problem results when the second spouse dies and assets are then transferred to the children. At that point, the estate tax credit comes into play.

Let us assume that Jane's father left his entire $2-million estate to Jane's mother when he died five years ago. His money passed to Jane's mother without any estate taxation due to the unlimited marital deduction. Jane's mother dies in 2011, leaving the full estate to Jane. The tax on $2 million in the year 2011 will have a top tax rate of 50 percent on assets over $1 million, reducing Jane's inheritance significantly.

If Jane's father and mother had planned better, Jane could have avoided paying that tax. Here's how. The assets are split evenly, so that $1 million is in his name and $1 million is in her name. When he dies, his $1 million goes to a credit shelter trust, not to his wife. His estate now comes under $1 million and therefore avoids taxation. Jane's mom's separate estate is worth $1 million. At her death, her taxable estate is $1 million, which also comes under the exclusion amount. So, the upshot of the estate planning is that the net estate that passes to Jane is $2 million.

The $1 million in the credit shelter trust assets are reasonably accessible to the surviving spouse. Typically in a credit shelter trust, the income from the trust goes to the spouse, with the principal or corpus going to the children.

> Put not your trust in money, but put your money in trust.
> ~ **Oliver Wendell Holmes**, Writer

The point of a credit shelter trust is to avoid estate taxes due when the second spouse dies. The strategy is to split assets between the spouses. When the first spouse dies, the assets go to the trust, rather than directly to the surviving spouse. The income from the trust can go to the surviving spouse, but essentially the principal is designated for the children. A qualified estate-planning attorney can draw up this type of trust to meet the IRS guidelines.

QTIP Trusts

Here is an ugly scenario that anybody would want to avoid: Bill and Lisa are married, with children from previous marriages but no children together. This is Bill's third marriage and Lisa's second. Bill and Lisa live in a house that Lisa owned before they married. Lisa put Bill on the title to the house. When she died, the house title went to Bill. He remarried and never again spoke to her children. They were forgotten, and when Bill died the house went to his own children.

A legal solution to that problem exists, and it is the Qualifying Terminal Interest Property (QTIP) trust.

With second marriages, in which spouses may have differing priorities about which children will inherit property, these differences can become accentuated after the death of one of the spouses. Often this can mean that the deceased spouse's children are deprived of their inheritance. A QTIP trust deals with this problem by allowing you to designate who will receive your house after your spouse dies. Your attorney writes the trust so that your spouse can live in the house according to the terms of the trust. While he has the benefit of the property, however, he does not control its disposition at his death; that control lies with the terms of the trust document you have written. One attractive feature of a properly written and executed QTIP trust is that the property can qualify for the unlimited marital deduction, but you do not have to give your spouse control over who will eventually inherit the property.

> I'm proud of paying taxes. The only thing is, I could be just as proud for half the money.
> **~ Arthur Godfrey, Entertainer**

In order to qualify for the unlimited marital tax deduction, the QTIP trust must include certain provisions. The surviving spouse must receive all income from the property at least annually. He must be given a life estate, meaning that he has the benefit of the property until his death. The property cannot be directed to another person as long as the spouse is alive. The property must end up in the spouse's estate on the spouse's death; this assures that the property will, eventually, be subject to estate taxation.

The Emotional Dimension of Wills and Trusts

Wills and trusts create a legal structure that helps families avoid conflict and acting out. They do this by making rules and boundaries that set limits around the financial life of the family, and by requiring the family to plan for the future. It can be tempting to avoid creating a will and any appropriate trusts, as they force us to deal with death, property, taxes, family loyalties, and other anxiety-producing issues. When we take the time, effort, and emotional energy to deal with these life issues head on, however, we ultimately ease everybody's anxiety by building a structure that addresses issues affecting all family members.

When a death happens and the appropriate estate planning has not been done, any family is at increased risk of serious emotional and financial injury. On the other hand, when you have done your estate planning with care, openness, and fairness, you will have done a great deal to foster harmony in your family. What better legacy could you leave for your family than that?

> People living deeply have no fear of death.
> ~ Anaïs Nin, Author

THE FOUR PHASES OF YOUR ECONOMIC LIFE CYCLE

18

In adulthood, your Economic Self goes through changes just as your Physical Self does. We have identified four phases in the lifecycle of your Economic Self. They are:

1. Launching Phase—Planting the Seeds
2. Establishing Phase—Buds Are Emerging
3. Prime Phase—Full Bloom
4. Harvesting Phase—Reaping the Benefits

In this chapter we will explore the challenges and developmental tasks of each phase.

Launching Phase—Planting the Seeds
AGE: MID-TWENTIES TO MID-THIRTIES

The first phase of the Economic Self is the Launching Phase. This period begins when you have finished your formal education and are beginning your career. This is a time of getting started—of planting the seeds for the harvest to come. Frequently there are young children on the scene during this phase.

James and Frank are a gay couple in Chapel Hill, North Carolina. They have an adopted son, Dylan, who is two years old. James just finished his psychiatric residency and has begun working at a psychiatric facility, making $135,000 per year. Frank is an artist, and is staying home

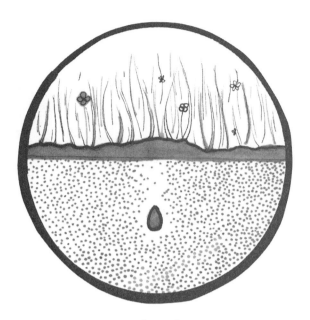

Launching Phase
"Planting the Seeds"

with Dylan until he begins kindergarten. They are both in their early thirties. The couple came to financial consultation to design a plan for themselves. Here are some of the goals that we arrived at in developing their financial plan:

- Fund James's 401(k) each month. They are starting with $1,000 monthly contribution. His employer matches up to 2 percent of his salary, which brings his annual 401(k) contribution to $14,700.
- Save for their first home. James and Frank are saving $1,250 each month for a down payment on their first home. They plan to save 10 percent before they buy. They will start with a condominium that should run about $300,000, and they plan to have the $30,000 down payment saved within two years.
- Pay down student loans. James and Frank have budgeted $600 per month to pay down student loans.

- Stay out of credit card debt. They are committed to a no-credit-card-debt policy; all cards are fully paid off each month.
- Purchase term life insurance. Both James and Frank have invested in $1,000,000 twenty-year term policies.
- Begin a 529 college savings plan for their son.
- Contribute an extra $300 monthly to the medical insurance provided by James's employer. This will give them full family coverage.

Because James and Frank are at the launching stage, and have more than thirty years before retirement, they have invested in an aggressive asset allocation. Here's a snapshot of their asset allocation:

> Financial instruments need to reflect the risk tolerance and life cycle people are in. Shop around before deciding where to place your savings.
> ~ Keith Leggett, Economist

Large-cap Value: 17 percent
Large-cap Growth: 13 percent
International Value: 11 percent
International Large-cap: 11 percent
Large-cap Blend: 11 percent
Mid-cap Value: 10 percent
Mid-cap Growth: 9 percent
Mid-cap Growth: 7 percent
Emerging Markets: 6 percent
Real Estate: 5 percent

James and Frank are a good example of young people dealing with the issues of the Launching Phase effectively. Let's take a look at some of the more typical issues. Debt from student loans frequently must be paid off in this phase. Buying a home and starting a college fund for the children are often on the agenda. Staying out of debt and developing a sense of economic responsibility are important tasks for people in this life phase. It is also necessary to consider the question of insurance: life insurance to protect dependent children and health insurance to cover the needs of a growing family. With the pressing concerns of the present, it can be difficult to look ahead. Nevertheless, the Launching Phase is the time to begin planning for the years to come. If your employer does not provide a 401(k), you would be well-advised to meet with a financial planner and put a retirement plan in place for yourself.

Emotional considerations

The Launching Phase is the time to set the trajectory of your economic life. No longer are you your parents' child. Your life is truly your own, and the steps you take now will lay a foundation for your comfort and security in later life. In your twenties it is nearly impossible to imagine that you will one day reach retirement age. Nevertheless, it is vital that you keep in mind the time value of money; money invested now will have several decades to work for you. When you reach midlife and retirement looms on the horizon, you will be grateful to your younger self for your foresight in taking responsibility for your financial future.

> The other day a man asked me what I thought was the best time of life. "Why," I answered without a thought, "now."
> ~ David Grayson, Journalist

Tips for Successfully Navigating the Launching Phase

- Begin your program of automatic investing in your retirement plan.
- Prepare to buy a home. Save for a down payment and go with a thirty-year fixed rate mortgage.
- Pay down student loans.
- Steer clear of credit card debt.
- Buy term life insurance if it's needed.
- Begin saving for children's college.
- Make certain you have health coverage, no matter how good your health.

Establishing Phase—Buds Are Emerging
AGE: MID-THIRTIES TO MID-FORTIES

The Establishing Phase is a time when the Launching Phase seeds begin to sprout—a kind of springtime of your eco-

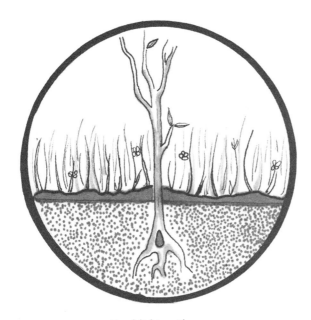

Establishing Phase
"Buds Are Emerging"

nomic life. If you haven't already done so, it's important to think seriously about buying your first home. Your earning power is beginning to increase, student loans are close to being paid off, and your retirement account is fattening.

Sheryl, thirty-eight, and Dave, forty-two, live in the Washington, DC, area. They are a good example of a couple who have met the challenges of the Launching Phase and are now well underway in the Establishing Phase. They have two children, Nancy, ten, and Clark, eight, and have recently bought a home. They have taken out a thirty-year fixed mortgage on their house but are actually hoping to have it paid off in twenty-one years. Each month they add 15 percent to their mortgage payment, which the bank uses to pay off principal. If they can continue doing this, they will save more than $129,000 dollars over the life of their $300,000 mortgage. Dave and Sheryl recognize the importance of staying out of debt. They have resisted buying on credit and calculate that their student loans should be paid off within three years. Planning for the children's future is a high priority for them. They have opened a 529 college savings plan for each of the kids, and both Dave and Sheryl hold a variable universal life insurance policy.

Because they are in the Establishing Phase and have about twenty-five years before they retire, Sheryl and Dave can be moderately aggressive in their asset allocation in both their retirement accounts and in the variable universal life policies. Their financial planner helped them invest in mutual funds that have a long record of good management and reasonable expense ratios. Here's the moderately aggressive asset allocation for Dave's individual 401(k):

Large-cap Value: 15 percent
Large-cap Growth: 10 percent
Large-cap Blend: 10 percent
International Value: 9 percent
International Large-cap: 9 percent
Mid-cap Value: 8 percent
Managed Bond: 8 percent
Inflation Managed Bond: 7 percent
Mid-cap Growth: 7 percent
Mid-cap Growth: 5 percent
Emerging Markets: 5 percent
Real Estate: 4 percent
Short Duration Bond: 3 percent

Clearly, Dave and Sheryl are a couple who value planning for the future over conspicuous consumption. Let's take a look at what they are doing right.

- They have bought a home within their means, and they have a fixed rate mortgage.
- They picked a home in an excellent school district, allowing them to avoid the ongoing expense of private schools.

> Success consists of a series of little daily victories.
> ~ Laddie F. Hutar,
>   Business Consultant

- They have worked out a realistic budget for luxuries—dining out, entertainment, and travel—and make every effort to stay within it.
- They have protected themselves and their children by purchasing appropriate insurance.
- They take satisfaction in watching their investments grow and knowing that the time value of money is working for them.

Emotional considerations

In the Establishing Phase it can feel like you are being stretched in every possible direction. There is always more being asked of you than you can manage. In this phase, it is vitally important not to neglect self-care. It is all too common for people in the Establishing Phase to substitute expensive luxuries for what they really need: rest, solitude, family time, fun with friends. Don't let yourself fall into this trap. You are working hard at this phase of your life, and you deserve to nourish and refresh your body and soul. Often this can require little or no money. Before you pull out your credit card, ask yourself a couple of questions:

- What is it I'm really longing for right now?
- Will making this purchase give me what I'm longing for?
- Will the true price of this purchase (an argument with my spouse, an overextended credit card, etc.) cancel out any possible benefits?
- Can I get what I'm really wanting by spending less money—or even none?

Just as seedlings need tender care until they grow into mature plants, so do our economic seedlings need care in the Establishing Phase. Paying attention now will allow you to enjoy the full bloom of the Prime Phase.

> Nothing comes easily that is done well.
> ~ Harry F. Banks, Writer

Tips for Successfully Navigating the Establishing Phase

· Pay off student loans.
· Look into buying a home with a fixed rate mortgage.
· Begin college savings for your children.
· Fund your retirement plan consistently and generously.
· Purchase life insurance as appropriate.

Prime Phase—Full Bloom
AGE: MID-FORTIES TO MID-/LATE-SIXTIES
By the time you have reached the Prime Phase—if you have planted and tended your seeds—you are beginning to enjoy a blooming economic garden. Along with enjoying the booms, however, it continues to be important to tend the crops. Remember, you will be living on the harvested benefits during the Harvesting Phase. At this point you either have or will soon have an empty nest. You and your children will reap the rewards of the college savings plan that you have funded, your earnings are at their peak, and you are looking toward retirement.

Hiroshi and Katie live in Sacramento, California. Hiroshi, age fifty-five, is an engineer with a small firm. Katie, age fifty, works for the state of California. They have three children, two already in college and one a high school senior. Hiroshi and Katie have saved for their children's education and have agreed to provide each of them support through four years of college. The couple's house will be paid off in five years, well before Hiroshi plans to retire at age sixty-five. Since Hiroshi's retirement is about ten years away, he and Katie have a moderately conservative asset allocation in his 401(k). Here's a snapshot of Hiroshi's moderately conservative asset allocation:

Managed Bond: 20 percent
Short Duration Bond: 17 percent
Inflation Managed Bond: 14 percent
Large-cap Value: 11 percent

Prime Phase
"Full Bloom"

Large-cap Blend: 7 percent
International Value: 6 percent
International Large-cap: 6 percent
Mid-cap Value: 5 percent
Large-cap Growth: 5 percent
Mid-cap Growth: 5 percent
Money Market: 4 percent

Hiroshi and Katie have not inherited family money nor has their income ever been particularly large. Nevertheless, they have been quite successful in their financial lives—not through making huge sums of money, but by using intelligence, common sense, and foresight about money.

- They own all three of their cars outright.
- Credit cards are paid off monthly.
- When they are poised to purchase a big-ticket item such as a car or a trip to visit Hiroshi's family in Japan, they

Every day you may make progress. Every step may be fruitful. Yet there will stretch out before you an ever-lengthening, ever-ascending, ever-improving path. You know you will never get to the end of the journey. But this, so far from discouraging, only adds to the joy and glory of the climb.
~ **Winston Churchill**

wait until they are able to pay with cash rather than buying on credit.

- They have instilled the values of financial responsibility in their children. Since adolescence, the children have had summer jobs and have been responsible for increasing portions of their own expenses.
- They have recently purchased long-term care insurance, with a policy that covers in-home care as well as care in a nursing facility.
- In four years, their twenty-year term policy will expire. At that point, their children will be independent and the need for life insurance will no longer be pressing.

Emotional considerations

Midlife can be a time of great satisfaction and enjoyment. However, it can also bring upheaval and difficulty. Be aware that the negative aspects of your money script will tend to show up in times of difficulty or stress. In the Prime Phase it is often especially important to deal with emotional and relationship issues. As we find we need to invest less energy in building a career or maintaining our family, it can be an opportunity for exploring our inner lives and enriching our relationships. Though this work may require some financial investment (in psychotherapy, life coaching, or couples work, for instance), it can be money well-spent. Truly knowing ourselves and strengthening the bonds with our loved ones will help us avoid the trap of foolhardy investing or overspending.

Tips for Successfully Navigating the Prime Phase

- If possible, pay off your home mortgage.
- Make sure that your asset allocation becomes more conservative as you get closer to retirement.
- Consider purchasing long-term care insurance by the time you reach your mid-fifties.

- Encourage your adult children to become financially independent as a gift to both them and you.
- Fund your retirement plan fully so that you will be well-prepared for a secure retirement.

Harvesting Phase—Reaping the Benefits
AGE: MID-/LATE-SIXTIES AND ONWARD

To be older, filled with wisdom, financially secure, and enjoying the fruits of a life well-lived—now that is something to look forward to! Working consciously on your Economic Self in the earlier phases prepares you for a Harvesting Phase that is fulfilling and rewarding. This is the time when you live on the bounty you have created in the earlier phases. You are reaping the harvest of a lifetime of commitment.

In the Harvesting Phase, it is vital to feel a sense of economic security and choice. Many people choose to work into their seventies, but working in your seventies is much more pleasant if you are doing it by choice rather than by necessity. With the body slowing down, a major focus of the Harvesting Phase is finding the right balance between work and rest, involvement and introspection. The Economic Self is ideally secure enough by now so that you can rely on the structures you created in the earlier phases.

In the Harvesting Phase there is an awareness of one's mortality, and this brings elders more fully than ever into life. As an elder friend of ours shared with us, "How do you live with yourself and others knowing that you won't be here forever? I'm paying attention to how I can play more, how to give back, how to love people fully, and yet be able to let them go."

From a financial planning point of view, the key factor in the Harvesting Phase is cash flow. Since many seniors live on a fixed income, it is vitally important to keep expenses well-below income in the older years. As we have emphasized earlier, one of the most effective ways to do this is to assure that your home mortgage is paid in full.

> By the age of fifty, you have made yourself what you are, and if it is good, it is better than your youth.
> ~ Marya Mannes, Journalist

Harvesting Phase
"Reaping the Benefits"

Betty is a seventy-three-year-old retired photographer. She had a studio with her husband, Chuck, until he passed away three years ago. She has two adult children and four grandchildren. Betty and Chuck paid their home off when they were sixty-five and contributed faithfully each month to their retirement fund, a SEP IRA that was worth $850,000 when she retired last year. She receives $1,415 per month in Social Security benefits. Last year she took $500,000 out of her SEP IRA and purchased an immediate annuity, which now provides her with $3,850 per month in income for the rest of her life. She has a variable universal life insurance policy with a death benefit of $1,000,000, which is paying for itself with money saved up in its cash value. Betty pays premiums each month to maintain her long-term care insurance.

She keeps her expenses down, and with her mortgage paid off, she lives quite comfortably on her fixed income. She owns a Medicare supplemental insurance policy and participates in the new Medicare Prescription Drug Program. She has updated her will and set in place advanced medical directives that make it clear that she does not want to be kept alive with machines should she become unable to make medical decisions on her own.

After purchasing the annuity to provide for lifetime income, Betty still has $350,000 in her SEP IRA. Here is the conservative asset allocation she has in her portfolio:

> Short Duration Bond: 28 percent
> Managed Bond: 26 percent
> Inflation Managed Bond: 16 percent
> Money Market: 8 percent
> Large-cap Blend: 6 percent
> Large-cap Value: 5 percent
> Large-cap Growth: 4 percent
> International Value: 3 percent
> Mid-cap Value: 2 percent
> International Large-cap: 2 percent

> Old age, especially an honored old age, has so great authority that this is of more value than all the pleasures of youth.
> ~ **Marcus Tullius Cicero, Ancient Roman Statesman**

With a guaranteed income from her annuity and social security, and her expenses reduced with her home mortgage paid off, Betty has succeeded in creating an excellent scenario for herself in her Harvesting Phase.

Emotional considerations

The Harvesting Phase is a time of integration and wisdom, when the learning of a lifetime comes together. Part of that wisdom comes from the experience of loss: the inevitable death of peers and loved ones. For the Economic Self, this is a time of reaping the crops that have been so carefully tended to over a lifetime. Difficulties arise when, for one reason or another, we have gotten derailed in our financial work, and fear for our economic well-being takes hold. In these circumstances, it is important to stay connected with our loved ones and not to isolate ourselves from others. It is also important to stay creative, as new and imaginative ways to solve economic problems can emerge through creative thinking. For example, we have a friend who went through some rocky times in her sixties and was left with only her social security check for financial sustenance in her Harvesting Phase. We encouraged her to discuss the issue with her family. She did so, and now she is living happily with her widowed sister. Pooling their resources has made life better for both of them. Throughout the life cycle we are always connected to others, and this is never more true than in the Harvesting Phase.

Tips for Successfully Navigating the Harvesting Phase

- Reduce expenses.
- Pay off your home mortgage.
- Choose a retirement age to start receiving Social Security benefits.
- Align the asset allocation in your portfolio with the goal of generating income rather than growth.
- Attend to advanced medical directives.
- Generate income from annuities.
- Update your will.
- Attend to estate planning issues to minimize taxation on your estate.
- Give gifts of money to family members.
- Be sure to have medical insurance with Medicare supplemental insurance.

Financial Success Throughout the Life Cycle

We have seen in this chapter that financial planning is a life-long journey. It is rewarding on every level to consciously work with your Economic Self. Once you are aware of all of the growth and learning that working on your Economic Self can offer, you will find that it is truly fascinating, even fun, to steer your way through all the changes and challenges of economic life. Tending to our economic well-being

A stock broker urged me to buy a stock that would triple in price every year. I told him, "At my age I don't even buy green bananas."
~ Claude D. Pepper, U.S. Senator

In 2006, you could give up to $12,000 to someone other than your spouse without having to pay gift taxes. For more information, go to *www.insightfulgroup.com*. Click on the Tax Center link and go to publication 950, Introduction to Estate and Gift Taxes.

allows us to grow emotionally and spiritually. Each phase, met with courage and commitment, offers a fresh opportunity for growth and integration.

Exercise: Taking Inventory

As you read through the information on the four phases, you probably developed a picture of where you are in your own life. It's unlikely that you will fit all the parameters of any one phase, but ask yourself which seems to be the best fit for you. While you reflect, consider your chronological age, your career stage, your family stage, and your financial position.

Once you have decided, it's time to take inventory. The objective here is not to berate yourself if you don't measure up to the description of the "ideal" couple described in each phase. Rather it's to begin to map out where you are and where you'd like to go on your path toward True Wealth. What have you already accomplished? What seems like the most important next step for you? What details in your home, career, or financial life do you need to focus on? Write freely in your Money Journal as the feelings and thoughts arise.

Now that you are familiar with each of the four phases of your economic life cycle and the tips for successfully navigating each one, you may find that setting up an appointment with a financial planner can be an enormous help (see the appendix for tips on choosing a financial planner). Even if you only ask for a few hours of consultation, a qualified financial planner can help you develop a road map that will stand you in good stead as you move through the changes and challenges of the life cycle phases.

> And in the end, it's not the years in your life that count. It's the life in your years.
> ~ **Abraham Lincoln**

PUT IT ALL TOGETHER:
Honoring Feelings, Understanding Patterns, Acting with Wisdom and Consciousness

19

You have seen throughout *True Self, True Wealth* that money—and how you deal with it—is central to your life. In working with your money issues, you have the opportunity to gain insight into yourself, your family of origin, your spirituality, your relationships, and your work. You learn about self-support and empowerment. You learn to honor your feelings. You learn that finding your economic power goes hand in hand with finding your spiritual and emotional power. Most of all, you learn that True Wealth can emerge only when you are operating out of True Self.

Though it may seem like a paradox, you must be in touch with your emotions before you can act *rationally* in the financial sphere. No longer do people whose strengths lie in the emotional/relational sphere need to feel at a disadvantage in the financial dimension. It is exactly these strengths that will serve you well in developing True Wealth. It is through honoring your emotions and allowing them to inform you that you develop the capacity to deal effectively with your financial life.

As you have worked with the concepts and done the exercises throughout this book, you have deepened your understanding of yourself and developed an increased ability to move with confidence in the economic sphere. Let's review the concepts that will continue to support you as you go forward on your journey:

> When we grow in spiritual consciousness, we identify with all that is in the world—there is no exploitation. It is ourselves we're helping, ourselves we're healing.
> ~ Govindappa Venkataswamy, Physician

We who lived in concentration camps can remember the men who walked through the huts comforting others, giving away their last piece of bread. They may have been few in number, but they offer sufficient proof that everything can be taken from a man but one thing: the last of the human freedoms— to choose one's attitude in any given set of circumstances, to choose one's own way.

~ Viktor Frankl, M.D.,
  Austrian Psychiatrist,
  Holocaust Survivor

- We started with an understanding of the Economic Self—the part of you that connects you to the world of money and finances. By allowing yourself to visualize what prosperity looks and feels like to you personally, you heal and strengthen your Economic Self.
- We have explored techniques for dismissing Superego Attacks when they arise. You know that the Superego attacks when you are vulnerable and creative—exactly the states so necessary for developing the Economic Self.
- We discussed the Paradoxical Theory of Change, which tells us that in order to change, we must be fully aware of how we really feel. Change comes as an organic out-growth of awareness. Inner scripts and unresolved emotional material can hamper your ability to choose prosperity.
- You identified your money script and became aware of the ways in which it limits you and can lead to self-defeating behavior. Being aware of your negative pat-terns allows you to choose those courses of action that will support the healthy growth of your Economic Self.
- You have increased your understanding of the ways in which healing the Economic Self is a deeply spiritual issue. In the old paradigm, you experience a painful split between yourself and the universe. You feel that there is only so much to go around—there is an agoniz-ing sense of separation and scarcity. As you heal the Economic Self, a new awareness of abundance emerges. You see that when you come consciously into your own power, economically and otherwise, you actually enrich the collective. It is in your fullness that you bring the most enrichment to our world.

As you move toward consciously manifesting your abun-dance, it is a natural impulse to give back. Philanthropy is not just for the wealthy; it is an expression of gratitude by all who experience abundance.

True Wealth begins with an understanding of the role of money in the history of your family. As you understand the economic struggles and successes of past generations, you come to a better understanding of yourself. Understanding your family's relationship to money is a first step in economic individuation, in which you become clear about your own economic values, goals, and challenges.

As you develop your Economic Self, you are free to act more lovingly and powerfully in your relationships with your partner and children. It is here, in the intimate sphere of life within your family, that your economic empowerment will be felt most strongly. Maintaining clear and loving communication around money with your partner will allow your whole family to flourish.

As you deal with questions of money, relationships, and family, you must also deal with creating healthy boundaries. Enmeshed boundaries can have serious financial consequences within any family system. Having healthy boundaries means being able to say "no" on financial issues with children, partners, friends, and extended family when "no" is the most appropriate answer. Healthy boundaries protect you from losing your sense of individuation and empowerment

> Feelings of worth can flourish only in an atmosphere where individual differences are appreciated, mistakes are tolerated, communication is open, and rules are flexible—the kind of atmosphere that is found in a nurturing family.
> ~ **Virginia Satir, Family Therapist**

With a sense of emotional grounding, empowerment, and healthy boundaries, you are able to support the life-long work of building and maintaining wealth. The first step in this process is to "fund your future first," which means you automatically fund a tax-advantaged retirement plan each month.

It is important to know how to invest. Your retirement funds should be invested in a tax-advantaged account. We recommend mutual funds, specifically well-managed funds with low expense ratios. You can then design an asset allocation according to your preferences, life goals, and needs. We suggest that you work with a qualified financial planner in putting your portfolio together.

Smart investors stay invested in their mutual fund portfolio even when markets go up and down. Many fortunes have been lost by investors trying to buy low and sell high. They usually end up doing just the opposite: buying high and selling low. Stick with your asset allocation—don't chase hot stocks or hot stock sectors. It can be tempting to sell when the stock market goes south, or to buy when the market is hot. Resist that temptation. Slow and steady wins the race when it comes to building and holding onto wealth.

Another aspect of building wealth is building home equity. Establish yourself with a traditional fixed-rate thirty-year mortgage, and pay an extra 15 percent each month to pay down principal early. You'll save money in the long run and take years off your mortgage. Owning your home is an excellent goal for retirement, as it will do a great deal toward decreasing your living expenses.

Earning is another area where you can do much to improve your financial position. Revising your self-concept and your expectations so that you learn to negotiate for what you are really worth will allow you to make more money for what you do. Earning more is a cornerstone of empowering your Economic Self. Learning your true worth and expecting to receive fair value for what you offer can help transform your whole sense of yourself.

Of course, with increased earning can come the temptation to spend it all. It is vitally important to stay conscious about your spending and to work on emotional issues in your relationships without spending. Real comfort in the end comes from relationships, not from things. Paying credit cards off each month keeps you out of the hole and allows you to use your money to enhance your own financial well-being rather than that of the credit card company.

A wise choice when it comes to cars is to buy a late-model used car. Don't lease, as leasing does nothing to help you build equity in your car. Get good insurance coverage—well above the minimums in your state—but shop around for the best price.

> Man's mind, once stretched by a new idea, never regains its original dimensions.
> ~ Oliver Wendell Holmes, Jurist

Why do wealthy people own insurance? Why, for example, does Bill Gates have a homeowners' policy? Surely he can afford to pay for any damage. It's because he wants to pass the risk to an insurance company. Insurance means that you are contracting with an insurance company to cover certain risks in your life. Health coverage is a necessity. Insurances that cover disability and long-term care are also important to consider at the appropriate times in your life. Life insurance comes in a variety of forms, but it is certainly necessary if you have dependents who need your financial support.

Estate planning involves preparing the way for those who will survive you. When done well, it allows you to take charge of how the wealth you have accumulated will be distributed after your death. It offers you an opportunity to provide for your family and contribute to causes that feel important to you. Making sure that it all does not go to the tax collector is a primary goal. Another important goal is making sure that your family knows your wishes regarding end of life issues should you become unable to express them yourself.

The economic life cycle has four phases, each with its unique set of financial objectives and challenges:

- Launching Phase
- Establishing Phase
- Prime Phase
- Harvesting Phase

The earlier phases deal with creating the financial structures of your life such as starting your retirement plan, buying a home, and getting established in your work so that you are making money sufficient to fund your life goals. The later phases follow through with your goals and set up a comfortable retirement.

Building True Wealth is an important way of connecting with the world. You learn to value yourself and see yourself

> Well-being is attained by little and little, and nevertheless is no little thing itself.
> ~ Zeno of Citium, Ancient Hellenistic Philosopher

as a precious part of all that is. You learn how to work with anxiety and how to facilitate change. You learn how to manage your relationships with both love and borders. You learn how to keep the money you make and put it to work to provide opportunity for yourself and your family.

It is our deepest hope that our journey together is a step forward on a path of fulfillment and joy for you.

May you find your own True Wealth.

May you bring your talents fully into the world.

May you help to heal the world with all that you have to give.

> Know thyself.
>
> ~ **Plato**

APPENDIX:
How to Choose a Financial Planner

For most people, it makes good sense to work with a qualified financial planner, as there really is no substitute for the professional relationship you develop with someone who understands the issues and can be your financial advocate. Probably the best way to find a reputable financial planner is to ask people you respect in your personal and professional networks if they are working with a financial planner they are happy with, and then interview the planner. If you choose to work with a financial planner, here are some steps to take to help ensure that he or she is highly qualified.

- Look for someone with advanced training and qualifications. ChFC (Chartered Financial Consultant) and CFP (Certified Financial Planner) are the two most widely accepted professional designations for financial planners. The ChFC designation is administered by the American College in Bryn Mawr, Pennsylvania. The CFP designation is administered by the CFP Board of Standards in Denver, Colorado. ChFCs and CFPs have taken a comprehensive curriculum in financial planning and have met specific experience, continuing education, and ethical requirements. Some CPAs have earned a financial planning designation called the PFS (Personal Financial Specialist), which consists of a comprehensive financial planning curriculum on top of the usual CPA requirements.

• Financial planners are paid in one of three ways—or often in combination: by commission, fee based on assets under management, or fee for service such as a yearly or hourly fee. At our firm, we prefer to work with fee based on assets under management, as we feel that approach aligns our financial interests with our clients and that it provides a sound financial framework for providing our professional services. Too many financial planning clients have no idea how their financial planner is paid. Whatever your financial planner's method of getting paid is, he or she should make it clear to you. Make sure that your financial planner is willing to discuss how he or she is paid and that the fee is transparent and not mysterious to you.

• Most financial planners are not "stock pickers" nor should they be. Stock brokers or money managers play an extremely important role in your financial plan, but the role of your financial planner should be to find you highly qualified money managers for each asset class you are invested in. If your financial planner is taking the time that he should to consult with you and other clients, then he is not taking the time to research investments as thoroughly as a dedicated money manager should be. Commonly recognized money managers run large mutual funds. With mutual funds and other instruments where many investors' money is pooled, the money manager earns his or her fee by taking a very small percentage of a very large pool of money so that the cost to the individual investor is kept low.

• Be wary of the financial salesman who calls you frequently with stock tips. This may be a sign that he is making transactions to generate commissions that are in his self-interest but not necessarily in the your best interest. In the industry, this form of unethical conduct is called "churning." Also be wary of the stock tip that is generated by the Wall Street firm that is both performing investment banking services for a given corporation and then sending its sales force out to sell the company's stock. If you have been reading the newspapers lately, you know that this type of client abuse has been all too common at some of the major brokerage houses in recent years, and although the brokerage firms have pledged to stop such abuses, it is best for you, the consumer, to be informed that these unethical practices have occurred in the recent past and could well occur again in the present and future. If you are getting frequent calls about hot stock tips from a financial salesman who is managing your money, it may be time to start looking for a professional financial planner who will take a holistic view of your financial well-being and who will not try to ply you with offers that are not in your best interest.

• Look for a financial planner who will meet with you regularly; who is willing to take the time to teach, listen; and who has good interpersonal skills. Dealing with the financial dimension of life causes many people a high degree of anxiety. Therefore, the ideal financial planner will have the technical facility to give state-of-the-art financial advice along with a capacity for helping clients contain their anxiety so as to make sound financial choices.

• Ask for references and take the time to call them. Other clients can tell you a lot about your prospective financial planner's interpersonal skills, technical skills, organization, and professional demeanor.

Finding a qualified financial planner that you are compatible with is an important step on your pathway to prosperity. Take your time in carefully choosing the financial planning professional who feels right for you.

GLOSSARY

401(k): A retirement plan that is funded by employee contributions and often with matching contributions from the employer. The contributions are taken pre-income tax and grow tax-free until money is withdrawn. Please see Individual 401(k).

403(b): A retirement plan for public schools, colleges, and certain nonprofits. These plans are self-directed. The employee makes a contribution which is sometimes matched by employer contribution. Tax-Sheltered Annuities are 403(b)s.

529 Plan: State-sponsored college savings plans that provide tax-advantaged college investing. Each state has a 529 program set up; your state may also provide you with state income tax advantages if you use your own state's plan. You can use any state's plan for the federal income deferral.

Amortization: The repayment of a loan (frequently used in reference to a mortgage) by the systematic repayment of interest and principal. In the early years of a mortgage, most of the payment goes to the payment of principal. An amortization schedule shows the pay-down of principal and the payment of interest with each mortgage payment over the life of the mortgage.

Annual Percentage Rate (APR): The Truth in Lending Act requires that lenders show the relationship of total

Thanks to Routledge (NY) for use of this material, originally published in *Mastering the Financial Dimension of Your Practice: The Definitive Guide to Private Practice Development and Financial Planning* (2004) by Peter Cole and Daisy Reese

finance charges associated with a loan. APR allows consumers to compare loans offered by competing lenders on equal terms, taking into account interest rates, points, and other finance charges as expressed in an annual percentage rate.

Annuitant: When an annuity contract is set up to make a regular payment to the policy holder, the policy holder who receives the annuity payments is the annuitant.

Annuity (Fixed): An annuity is a contract with an insurance company. The annuity provides for tax-deferred growth on savings in the funding phase. When the annuitant is ready to retire, the contract is then "annuitized," meaning that regular payments are made to the annuitant. Fixed annuities earn interest that is tax-deferred until withdrawn.

Annuity (Variable): Variable annuities provide for tax-deferred growth in separate accounts during the funding phase and payment on growth in the annuity when paid out. Variable annuities invest the policy-holder's money in securities such as stocks and bonds that vary in value.[1]

Appreciation: Refers to the increase in the value of an asset. For example, a stock that you bought at one price a year ago may have appreciated to a higher price today. Appreciation also commonly refers to real estate values.

Asset: An item you own that has value such as a stock, bond, real estate, or automobile.

Asset Allocation: A mixture of investments of various types that is designed to match the goals and preferences of the investor. Asset allocation models frequently vary

---

1 Variable annuities are sold by prospectus only. Investors should read the prospectus carefully before investing. Annuities are long-term investments designed for retirement purposes. Withdrawals of taxable amounts are subject to income tax and, if taken prior to age fifty-nine-and-a-half, a 10 percent federal tax penalty may apply. Early withdrawals may be subject to withdrawal

from conservative, moderately conservative, moderate, moderately aggressive, and aggressive.

Asset Class: A category of investment type such as stocks, bonds, real estate, or cash.

Bear Market: A period in which stock prices are declining. A bear market can last months or even years.

Blue Chip Stocks: Equity issues of highly regarded companies that are well-established. Many blue chip companies pay dividends in both bull markets and bear markets.

Bonds: A formal certificate of debt issued by a government entity or corporation. Most bonds make a fixed payment at regular intervals, which is normally a fixed percentage of the face value of the bond. The face value is repaid when the bond matures.

Bull Market: A period in which stock prices are rising. A bull market can last months or even years.

Cash: Cash is not just the money you have in your wallet or in the bank. As an asset class, cash refers to treasury bills, short-term commercial paper, high-quality municipal debt, high-quality short-term corporate debt, and other high-quality short term securities. Cash has the lowest volatility of all asset classes. See money market funds.

Cash Equivalents: Cash equivalents include money market funds, T-bills, and CDs.

Cash Surrender Value: The value of funds returnable at any given time to the insured upon the immediate surrender of a policy. Most life insurance and annuity contracts have significant deferred sales charges, making

---

charges. An investment in the securities underlying a variable annuity involves investment risk, including possible loss of principal. The contract, when redeemed, may be worth more or less than the original investment. The purchase of a variable annuity is not required for, and is not a term of, the provision of any banking service or activity. Guarantees are backed by the claims-paying ability of the issuer.

the cash surrender value less than the cash value. For this reason, such contracts only make sense if you are in them for the long haul.

Cash Value: The value of the savings element in permanent insurance.

Certificate of Deposit (CD): CDs are low-risk investments offered by banks for varying durations up to five years. CDs are generally insured by the FDIC up to $100,000 per depositor and banking institution. Fees are usually assessed for early withdrawal.

Charitable Remainder Trust (CRT): An irrevocable trust with one or more living income beneficiaries and one or more qualified exempt charitable organizations to receive the remainder of the trust upon expiration of the income interest. CRTs are often used with highly appreciated securities. A properly structured CRT permits the donor to receive income, estate, and/or gift-tax advantages.

Chartered Financial Consultant (ChFC): The ChFC designation has been conferred on more than 40,000 financial professionals since its inception in 1982. ChFC designees have completed a comprehensive curriculum in financial planning and have met specific experience and ethical requirements.

Common Stock: A security that represents ownership in a corporation. Shares are bought by the stockholder who can, in turn, sell the share in a stock exchange.

Compounding: A process whereby the value of an investment increases by using the principal plus the previously earned interest to calculate interest payments. Compound interest contrasts with simple interest, which bases interest payments simply on the original principal without including previously earned interest to calculate present interest payments.

Conservator: A guardian and protector appointed by the court to protect and manage the financial affairs and/or the daily life of an individual who is not capable of managing his or her own affairs due to physical or mental limitations.

Consumer Debt: Debt that is incurred in the purchase of consumer goods, such as credit card debt, auto loans, and store financed debt. Unlike most mortgage debt, most consumer debt is not deductible.

Corporate Bond: A formal debt security issued by a corporation. Most corporate bonds are offered with a $1,000 face value. Generally corporate bonds pay higher coupon than government bonds because of higher risk. Corporate bonds are rated for risk by independent rating agencies. As a general rule, the higher the risk, the higher the coupon rate of the bond.

Corporation: Legal structure for a business to act as an artificial person that can sue or be sued. A for-profit corporation may issue shares of stock to raise funds.

Custodial Care: A term used in long-term care and long-term care insurance that refers to caring for personal needs such as walking, bathing, dressing, eating, or taking medicine. Medicare does not pay for custodial care.

Debt Markets: The exchanges where debt securities such as U.S. government bonds, municipal bonds, and corporate bonds are bought and sold.

Decedent: A legal term used in life insurance and estate planning for a person who has died.

Defined Benefit Pension Plan: A pension plan in which the employer assumes investment risk and specifies the amount that will be paid to the employee in retirement. Such plans commonly provide a formula for the amount paid in retirement as calculated by the number of years served in relation to salary received. Such plans are expensive for employers and are becoming less common in the private sector than they were in years past, although such plans are still common in public employment.

Defined Contribution Plan: In such plans, the employee assumes investment risk. The employer does not guarantee a given amount of income in retirement. Instead, contributions are made into the plan and benefits are received based on contributions made into the plan, performance of investments made by the plan, and vesting. These plans are considered less costly than defined benefit plans for employers.

Depreciation: Depreciation is an accounting technique that represents the decline in value of an asset over time. For tax purposes, a business owner writes off the cost of an asset over a period of time with charges made against earnings.

Disability Insurance: A policy designed to pay benefits based on a percentage of earned income if the insured becomes unable to work. Disability insurance is distinct from long-term care insurance and does not cover the same risks.

Disposable Income: Income that is available for spending or saving after taxes have been paid.

Diversification: An investment strategy to spread risk among a variety of investments such as stock mutual funds, bonds, real estate, individual stocks of a variety of companies, and so on. The goal of diversification is to not put all your eggs in one basket so that factors that may adversely affect one of your holdings will not have an adverse effect on all of your holdings.

Dividends: A portion of a company's profit that is distributed to its shareholders. Dividend-paying companies are frequently large and well-established.

Dollar Cost Averaging: A method of investing a fixed amount of money into an investment such as a mutual fund. Frequently, the money is transferred directly from a bank account into the investment on a monthly basis without regard to the price of the investment. The investor buys more shares when the price is low and fewer shares when the price is high. This may result in lowering the average cost per share. Dollar cost averaging neither guarantees a profit nor eliminates the risk of losses in declining markets, and you should consider your ability to continue investing through periods of market volatility and/or low prices.

Dow Jones Industrial Average (DJIA): A widely used indicator of the stock market, the DJIA has been computed since 1896. It is a price-weighted average of thirty blue chip companies chosen by the *Wall Street Journal*. The DJIA currently includes GE, GM, HP, Coca-Cola, Microsoft, and Exxon/Mobile.

Durable Power of Attorney for Healthcare: A durable power of attorney for healthcare empowers the person you appoint to make healthcare decisions for you. You designate a person who makes medical decisions for you if you are unable to make them due to illness or incapacity. Most people choose a family member or close friend to act as the decision maker.

Equity: In the context of stocks, equity refers to an Ownership interest in a corporation in the form of common stock or preferred stock. In a real estate context, equity refers to the difference between the amount owed on the mortgage and the value of the property.

Estate: All that a person owns. Upon death, "estate" refers to the total value of the decedent's assets. The value of the decedent's estate includes all funds, interest in businesses, real property, real estate, stocks, bonds, notes receivable, and any other asset the person may have possessed.

Estate Planning: The orderly and thoughtful preparation of a plan to administer and dispose of one's property so that after death, the people and/or institutions that the decedent favors will receive maximum benefit with minimum loss of assets to taxes.

Estate Tax: Tax levied on the transfer of property from the decedent to his or her beneficiaries and heirs. It is based on the amount in the decedent's estate and can include insurance proceeds.

Executor: The person named in a will and appointed to carry out the desires of the decedent. Responsibilities include gathering up and protecting the assets in the estate, ensuring that heirs and beneficiaries are treated according to the terms of the will, making sure that estate debts are paid, and managing the calculation and payment of estate taxes.

Face Amount: The amount to be paid upon death or maturity of a life insurance policy.

Face Value: In the context of a debt security, the amount paid to the bondholder when the bond matures.

Fair Market Value: The amount that an asset would bring in the open market if put up for sale.

FICO: A FICO score is a credit score developed by Fair Issac & Co. Credit scoring is a method of determining the likelihood that credit users will pay their bills. Fair Issac began its pioneering work with credit scoring in the late 1950s.

Fiduciary: A party who holds assets and occupies a position of trust such as a trustee, executor, or retirement plan administrator.

Financial Advisor/Planner: A professional who assists individuals, families, and organizations in carrying out their financial goals.

Fixed Annuities: A contract between an annuity owner and an insurance company that can guarantee fixed payments over the life of the annuity. The annuitant can rely on a fixed stream of income with the insurance company assuming the investment risk.

Fixed Investment: An investment such as a bond, Certificate of Deposit, or note that pays a given rate of interest.

Fixed-Rate Mortgage: A loan on a property that is set and does not change over the life of the loan.

Fluctuation: The variation in prices of stocks and other securities traded in secondary markets.

Fund Manager: A person (or team) who is responsible for making investment decisions related to a mutual fund or other formal portfolio such as a pension or insurance fund.

Fundamental Analysis: A method of stock valuation that studies a company's financial statements, operations, earnings, competition, and management strength. Fundamental analysis focuses on the company itself and is contrasted by technical analysis.

Future Value: A calculation relating to the time value of money. It calculates money's value in the future given the present value of the money, the number of years it will be held, the percentage rate at which it will grow, the number of times interest will be compounded per year, and the amount and number of payments that will be added over the years it is to be held.

Group Insurance: Insurance issued to a group such as employees of a company or members of a credit union.

Growth Stock: A common stock whose price is considered likely to increase because the issuing company's business is poised for growth.

Guardian: Used in connection with wills and estate planning, this is a person named to care for another person, usually a minor.

Healthcare Advance Directive: A document that expresses your general wishes about your medical treatment, in the event that you cannot speak for yourself in the future. See Durable Power of Attorney for Healthcare.

Home Equity Loan: A loan that is collateralized with the equity the borrower has in his or her home. The interest paid on home equity loans is sometimes deductible as mortgage interest.

Illiquid: Assets that are not readily converted to cash such as real estate, collectibles, and limited partnerships.

Illustration: An insurance term for a projection of how a specific permanent insurance policy or annuity is expected to perform over time, given certain inputs such as rate of return, premium payments, and length of time that premium payments are made.

Income Stock: A stock that has consistently paid high dividends.

Individual 401(k): New 401(k) plans established with the 2001 tax law. These plans allow individuals in solo practice and their spouses to establish a 401(k) with greatly reduced administrative requirements. See 401(k).

Inflation: An economic term that describes a period in which there is an increase in the price of goods and services that causes a decline in purchasing power.

In-Force Policy: An insurance policy that is sufficiently paid up as to be currently in effect and valid.

Insurability: The degree to which an insurance company is willing and able to insure a particular person given his or her health status and other risk factors.

Insured: A person who is covered by a health, auto, or life insurance policy.

Interest Rate Risk: In a fixed investment, the risk that the interest being paid will be less than the going rate at a future date.

Intestate: To die intestate is to die without a will. In such cases, state law determines the disposition of an estate.

Investment Portfolio: A mixture of securities and other assets that is designed to meet the needs of the investor. Refers to looking at the entire collection of holdings in their totality.

Investment Strategy: The approach an investor employs in making his or her investment decisions.

Individual Retirement Account (IRA): If one meets certain requirements set forth by the IRS, an individual may fund a Traditional IRA with pre-tax dollars that will grow tax deferred and will be taxed when spent in retirement.

IRA Rollover: Certain retirement accounts may be "rolled over" into an Individual Retirement Account held at a financial institution. For example, an individual who separates from service with a school district may be eligible to roll his or her 403(b) retirement account into a rollover IRA. The IRS has specified certain rules and penalties with regard to IRA rollovers, so be sure to consult with a financial professional before you roll over your retirement account.

Junk Bonds: Bonds issued by entities that receive a below investment-grade rating from independent rating agencies such as Standard and Poors. Junk bonds must pay higher coupon rates than investment-grade bonds to attract investors.

Keogh: A tax-deferred retirement plan for self-employed individuals and the employees of sole proprietors. The Keogh is frequently used by sole proprietors for retirement saving.

Leverage: Debt. A company that is highly leveraged is using borrowed money. Similarly, an investor using leverage is using borrowed money in his or her investing. The use of borrowed money in investing increases risk and may magnify gains and/or losses.

Liability Insurance: Insurance that covers the possibility of loss due to being held responsible for another's injury caused by negligence or inappropriate action.

Life Expectancy: Based on actuarial tables, an insurance company's estimate of the insured's life span. Life expectancy is used in calculating life insurance premiums.

Life Insurance: Insurance that pays a specified amount on the death of the insured.

Liquidity: The degree to which an investment is readily convertible to cash without penalty or loss.

Living Will: Document that specifies one's wishes with regard to medical treatment in the event the individual becomes incapable of making his or her own medical decisions. Commonly, living wills state whether an individual does or does not want life support.

Long-Term Care: Custodial, intermediate, or skilled nursing care provided to an individual who does not need acute care but cannot independently handle the activities of daily living.

Long-Term Care Insurance: A type of health insurance specifically designed to cover long-term care expenses. Some policies cover home health care and assisted living expenses. Benefits are triggered when the insured cannot independently take care of specified activities of daily living.

Medicaid (Medi-Cal, in California): Medical expense benefits for individuals and families deemed to be low-income and otherwise eligible by state and federal guidelines.

Medical Power of Attorney: A document giving an individual (agent) the authority to make medical decisions on behalf of the person assigning the power of attorney in the event that he or she becomes incapable of making his or her own medical decisions. The agent is usually a trusted friend or relative.

Medicare: Federal program that provides medical expense benefits for retired Americans. Medicare Part A provides coverage for in-hospital acute care. Part B provides out-patient coverage.

Medi-gap Insurance: Insurance that covers some, but not all, areas of medical expense (gaps) uncovered by Medicare. Medi-gap insurance does not cover long-term care expenses. There are various levels of Medi-gap insurance that have been standardized by state insurance commissioners.

Minimum Distribution: In most tax-deferred retirement plans, there comes a point (age seventy-and-a-half for most plans) when the retiree must begin to take money out of the plan and pay taxes on the portion that comes out. The minimum amount the retiree must take out is known as the minimum distribution.

Money Manager: Investment professional who buys and sells securities on behalf of his clients for a fee.

Money Market Funds: Highly liquid and conservative funds that attempt to keep the value of one share to one dollar with interest rates that vary. These funds invest in short term debt obligations such as T-Bills, Commercial Paper, and CDs.

Mortality Tables: Actuarial charts that insurance companies use to predict life expectancy of an applicant or insured individual.

Mortgage-Backed Securities: Securities that are backed by pooled mortgages. Government National Mortgage Association (Ginnie Mae), Federal National Mortgage Association (Fannie Mae), and Federal Home Loan Mortgage Corporation (Freddie Mac) are three entities that issue such securities.

Municipal Bonds: Debt securities issued by state, county, and local government entities including water districts and school districts. "Munis" are typically not subject to federal income tax and therefore offer lower coupon rates than taxable bonds. Their lower coupon rate typically makes munis inappropriate investments in tax-deferred accounts.

Mutual Fund: Open-end investment company that combines the investment dollars of many shareholders to manage a portfolio of securities, typically stocks and/or bonds. Mutual funds are used by small investors and large investors alike. They offer instant diversification, professional management, and the cost savings of sharing transaction fees among the shareholders. Mutual funds are sold by prospectus. The prospectus informs potential and current shareholders about the investment focus, fees, management, and performance of the mutual fund.

National Association of Securities Dealers (NASD): Established under federal law, this is a private, not-for-profit organization dedicated to bringing integrity to the markets and confidence to investors. Virtually every securities firm doing business in the United States is a member of the NASD. Among other responsibilities, the NASD acts as a provider of financial regulatory services to the U.S. securities industry.

Net Asset Value (NAV): Mutual funds hold many securities. At the end of each trading day, mutual fund companies must compute the value of a single mutual fund share. This computation involves adding up the total value of the underlying assets, subtracting the funds liabilities, and then dividing by the number of shares outstanding.

Net Worth: An individual's total assets minus total liabilities equal his or her net worth.

Pension Plan: A qualified retirement plan. Defined benefit plans are more traditional pension plans that place the investment risk with the company and pay a specific amount in retirement based on factors such as years of service, previous salary, and vesting. Defined contribution plans, on the other hand, place the investment risk with the employee, and benefits are based accumulated account balances rather than a promise by the company to pay a specified amount. Popular defined contribution plans are 401(k)s and 403(b)s.

Policy: An insurance contract between a policy owner and an insurance company that sets forth the terms and conditions of insurance.

Policy Loan: In permanent life insurance, a loan to the policy owner by the insurance company that is secured by the cash value in the policy.

Power of Attorney: A document placing decision-making power in the hands of a trusted person to act on behalf of the individual signing over this decision-making power.

Preferred Stock: Dividend paying stock that is primarily held by corporations. Preferred stock takes precedence

over common stock in the event of bankruptcy and liq-
uidation. Dividends are paid to preferred stock before
they are paid to common stock.

Premium: The amount a policy holder pays the insurer to
keep a life insurance policy in force.

Principal: In a mortgage or other loan, the principal is the
outstanding amount owed other than interest. When a
payment is made, principal is the part of the outstanding balance that is thereby reduced. In an investment
account, principal is the amount originally invested.
When an investor says "I am not touching the principal,"
her or she is referring to leaving the original amount
invested in the account while leaving the option open to
take dividends or interest payments as income.

Probate: Administration of the estate of a deceased person
under the supervision of the court.

Profit-Sharing Plan: A qualified retirement plan that
allows individuals in private practice to put away a portion of their income on a pre-tax basis for retirement.
The funds will grow tax deferred, and will be taxed when
distributed in retirement. If you have employees, you
will have to contribute for them as well.

Prospectus: For mutual fund and variable product, separate account investing, this document is produced by an
investment company and must meet the specific guidelines of the Securities Exchange Commission in
describing in detail the investment being offered. The
prospectus provides terms, objectives, historical
returns, costs, biographical information, and other
information that is deemed useful in providing
prospective investors with information helpful in making informed decisions.

Qualified Retirement Plan: Qualified retirement plans are
authorized by the IRS to provide tax advantaged retirement investing. Qualified plans are offered through one's
employment. For sole proprietors in private practice, a

qualified plan such as a 401(k) or Keogh can be established with the individual in solo practice, acting both as employer and employee. Qualified plans require strict compliance with IRS rules, so it is advisable to seek professional advice in establishing and maintaining them.

Refinance: To take out a new loan on a home or commercial mortgage that replaces the old loan, presumably with more favorable terms to the borrower.

Registered Representative: A person who has passed the appropriate NASD tests and may sell securities as an agent through association with an NASD member broker/dealer.

Rider: An optional feature on an insurance policy. The policy holder may choose a rider that he or she feels is in his or her interest in exchange for a higher premium. Example: on a permanent life insurance policy, an accelerated death benefit rider would allow for early partial payment of the death benefit to the insured during his or her lifetime if certain conditions are met.

Roth IRA: An individual retirement account that is funded with after-tax dollars. Money may be withdrawn tax-free in retirement. In contrast, the Traditional IRA is funded with pre-tax dollars that are then taxed when distributed in retirement.

Rule of 72: A way to approximate when your money will double given a fixed annual compound interest rate. Divide 72 by the expected rate of return to approximate the number of years it will take to double your money. For example, if you are earning 5 percent compounded annually and you reinvest all of your interest, you will double your money in approximately 14.4 years.

S&P 500 Index: Standard and Poors identifies 500 well-established American corporations for inclusion in this widely regarded measure of large-cap U.S. stock market performance. The S&P 500 attempts to include a representative sample of leading companies in leading industries.

Safety of Principal: An investment objective emphasizing that the original amount invested be as protected as is feasible given the risk characteristics of a given portfolio. The more aggressive the portfolio, the less emphasis there is on safety of principal. Conversely, the more conservative the portfolio, the more emphasis is placed on safety of principal. Safety of principal is assured up to the limits of FDIC protection with accounts in depository institutions that are covered by the FDIC.

Second Mortgage: A loan, collateralized by real estate, that is in addition to the primary mortgage. It carries rights that are junior to those of the primary mortgage.

Securities Exchange Commission (SEC): The primary federal regulatory body for the securities industry. The SEC promotes full disclosure and is charged with preventing fraud and manipulative practices in the securities industry.

SEP IRA: A tax advantaged retirement vehicle. The Simplified Employee Pension IRA is commonly used by therapists in private practice for tax-advantaged retirement investing.

Skilled Nursing Care: In long-term care planning, the level of care needed by a patient who requires round-the-clock supervision by an RN.

Skilled Nursing Facility: A facility primarily engaged in providing skilled nursing care to its residents.

Small Cap: Small capitalization stocks are those of smaller, publicly traded companies. This asset category is generally more aggressive and growth oriented than the stocks of more established companies with larger capitalization.

Stock Dividend: The common stocks of certain companies regularly pay shareholders a portion of income earned called dividends. Although some common stocks customarily and regularly pay dividends, corporations are not legally obligated to pay dividends on common stock.

Stock Exchange: A market where stocks, bonds, and other equities are bought and sold. Major American stock exchanges include the New York Stock Exchange, the American Exchange, and the NASDAQ.

Stocks: A stock certificate signifies an ownership position or equity in a corporation. The amount of ownership the stockholder has in the corporation is proportional to the percentage of the stock he or she owns relative to total stock outstanding.

Surrender Value: In Variable Life Insurance or Variable Annuities, the surrender value is cash value of the policy minus any deferred sales and surrender charges. Most Variable Life Insurance and Variable Annuities have substantial surrender charges and are therefore only suitable for people who intend to hold the policy over the long-term.

Suitability: An investment's appropriateness for a particular investor given the individual's risk tolerance, financial circumstances, and life circumstances. Registered representatives are required by the NASD and SEC to only sell investments that are suitable for their client.

Tax Credit: A dollar-for-dollar, direct reduction that offsets other income tax liabilities. Certain investments offer tax credits as their primary selling point.

Tax Deduction: A reduction in total income relative to the individual's tax bracket. A tax deduction is subtracted from adjusted gross income in determining taxable income. Contributions to qualified plans, state and local taxes, and charitable gifts are common tax deductions.

Tax-Deferred: In tax-deferred accounts such as qualified plans, the contributions to the accounts go in on a pre-tax basis, and the taxation on the money is deferred until it is withdrawn in retirement.

Tax-Sheltered Annuity (TSA): Offered by certain non-profit organizations, school districts, and hospitals as tax-deferred retirement plans.

Tenants in Common: The holding of property by two or more people, usually a couple, each of whom have an undivided interest in their portion of the property. One person may sell his or her share or leave it in a will without the consent of the other owner or owners. If a person dies without a will, the share goes to the heirs, not to the other owners.

Term Life Insurance: Life insurance that has no cash value and is time-limited. Term life insurance is contrasted with permanent life insurance, which is priced to last until the insured's death, at which time it will pay a death benefit carrying a cash value. Term insurance is significantly less expensive than permanent insurance.

Testamentary Trust: A trust created under the provisions of a will. A testamentary trust takes effect upon the death of the grantor.

Ticker Symbol: A combination of letters that is shorthand for a security. Some famous ticker symbols include MSFT (Microsoft), GM (General Motors Corp.), JNJ (Johnson & Johnson), and GE (General Electric).

Time Value of Money: A calculation of compound interest over a given number of years with a given interest rate and given contributions. Time value of money refers to the concept that a given amount of money will be worth more in the future than it is now because of money's capacity to garner interest.

Total Disability: Some insurance policies define total disability as the inability of the insured to perform any work for which he/she is qualified. Other policies define total disability as the insured's inability to perform the duties of his or her own occupation. Some policies may change occupation definitions after a specified period of disability. In choosing a disability policy it is important to understand how your insurer defines total disability.

Treasury Bill: A debt security offered by the U.S. Department of Treasury that has a duration of less than one year.

Treasury Bond: A debt security offered by the U.S. Department of Treasury that has a duration of more than ten years.

Treasury Note: A debt security offered by the U.S. Department of Treasury that has a duration of between one and ten years.

Universal Life Insurance: A kind of permanent life insurance that offers flexibility of premium payments. Universal life offers a death benefit along with a tax-advantaged savings component. The policy holder may borrow against the cash value in the policy without paying taxes on the borrowed sum. As long as the policy stays in force, the loan need not be paid back. At the time of death, if a loan is outstanding, the death benefit will be reduced by the amount of the outstanding loan.

Unlimited Marital Deduction: In estate planning, the unlimited marital deduction refers to the fact that married people can leave unlimited assets to their spouses without incurring estate taxes. The estate taxes are eventually collected when the surviving spouse dies.

Value Stocks: Stocks that are thought to be a good buy primarily because the stock's price is considered to be under-priced when subjected to fundamental analysis of the earnings and overall health of the issuing corporation.

Variable Investment: An investment in a security that can gain or lose in value. Stocks and bonds are variable investments in that their value can and does vary when sold in the secondary stock and bond markets.

Variable or Adjustable Rate Mortgage: A mortgage whose rate changes with interest rates. Generally, variable rate mortgages are available at lower initial rates because the borrower is assuming the risk that rates will rise. In contrast, fixed rate mortgages are generally more expensive because the lender is assuming the risk that rates will rise.

Variable Universal Life Insurance: Life insurance that combines a death benefit with a tax-advantaged investment component. The insurer directs the investment among the separate accounts that are offered within the policy. The separate accounts are typically managed by the same money management firms that manage large mutual funds and pensions. The policy-holder may borrow against the cash value in the policy without paying taxes on the amount borrowed. The amount borrowed may not need to be repaid as long as the policy remains in force. If the insured dies with the policy in force and with borrowed funds outstanding, the death benefit is reduced by the outstanding loan amount. Variable Universal Life policies typically have steep deferred sales charges that decline and disappear over time. These polices are only appropriate for long-term investors.

Vesting: Retirement accounts frequently include both employee and employer contributions. Vesting refers to the schedule set out in the retirement plan by which the employee acquires ownership in the retirement funds contributed by the employer. Employee-contributed funds are always fully vested.

Viatical Settlement: If a person with a terminal illness such as cancer or AIDS owns a life insurance policy, that policy may be sold in a viatical settlement that gives the insured less than the death benefit for use while still living. The purchaser of the policy pays the premium and receives the death benefit on the insured's death. At the height of the U.S. AIDS epidemic in the 1980s, viatical settlements were commonly used by AIDS sufferers to meet their financial obligations.

Whole Life Insurance: Permanent insurance that has both a death benefit and a cash value that accrues over time.

Zero Coupon Bonds: Bonds that do not make regular coupon payments, but instead are sold at a discount and are paid face value at maturity.

INDEX

Note: The bold page numbers indicate glossary definitions. The page numbers followed with t indicate a table and followed with f indicate a figure or illustration.